Qualitative Research Online

Thomas W. Miller
Jeff Walkowski
EDITORS

Research Publishers LLC

Qualitative Research Online

Publisher
Research Publishers LLC
PO Box 45229
Madison, WI 53744–5229
USA
http://www.research-publishers.com

Project coordinated by Cathy Green; production managed by John Tauber.
Printed and bound by R. R. Donnelley and Sons, Allentown, Pa.

Printed in the United States of America. 9 8 7 6 5 4 3 2

ISBN 0-9727297-1-2

Contents

Appendices

Preface

Qualitative research online is a growth area. More than just a new technology or modality of research, qualitative research online represents a cultural change in the way that we do research and the way we think about research.

Things happen faster when we go online. We have access to networked resources. We have the computer to collect and analyze data. We take words from e-mail messages and online discussions and automatically convert them into transcripts for text analysis. Raw data are at our fingertips, a few mouse clicks away from our monitors, printers, and data analysis programs.

We are just beginning to understand the potential of qualitative research online for contributing to our knowledge of social and business phenomena. Several companies have entered the virtual focus group hosting and rental service business. Healthy competition exists among providers of online software and services. But obstacles must be overcome before qualitative research online will be fully accepted by the research community.

While many researchers recognize the time and cost advantages of online research, some decry its claimed methodological flaws. Many researchers are unaware of or misinformed about technology for online research. There is resistance from traditional qualitative researchers. There is concern that online methods may replace what some think of as more appropriate face-to-face methods.

Like traditional qualitative research, qualitative research online should be purposeful research. We watch what people do. We listen to what they say through their typing and clicking. We collect data and interpret those data. We try to be objective, knowing that what we learn from data is often guided by the subjective categories we impose upon those data. Qualitative research online, like all research, requires care in design, analysis, and interpretation.

We do not expect online methods to replace traditional methods; nor do we propose that online methods replace traditional methods. Face-to-face interviews, focus groups, case studies, field observation and ethnography—these remain important methods for learning about people and cultures. But qualitative research online has a role to play in the social sciences and business. What role can it play, and how can it play that role most convincingly or effectively? We address these questions with the help of research practitioners.

This book represents more than the personal views of two authors. Our views are supplemented by views from guided discussions among research practitioners. Diverse, informed, experienced, and insightful—the participants in our panel and bulletin board discussions are pioneers in qualitative research online. We thank them for leading us on the path to understanding this new and important class of research methods.

There are many excellent books about qualitative research. Our intent is not to duplicate or substitute for these. We do not attempt to describe the full range of qualitative endeavor, nor should we in this short book. We do not introduce new theory of qualitative analysis or interpretation. Our goal is to provide a balanced and critical review of qualitative research online and to place it within the broader context of qualitative research in the social sciences and business.

As a stand-alone introduction to qualitative research online, this book serves as a reference for practitioners. The book may also be used as a supplementary textbook in qualitative, social, and marketing research courses. Our goal is to promote education and research in online methods and to encourage the appropriate use of online methods.

The book introduces focused conversation, a method of qualitative research online developed by the first author. Initial field studies employing focused conversation have been conducted by Chamberlain Research Consultants of Madison, Wisconsin. Focused conversation is the data collection component of the *Automated Process for Large-Scale Qualitative Research* (Patent Pending) from Data Arts LLC.

We have many people to thank for helping in the production of this book. Ted Kendall (formerly of QualTalk.com) and Dan Weber and Jolene Vanthuyne of Itracks provided access to bulletin board software used in producing the discussion transcripts of Chapters 3 and 4. Steve Cook and Siobhan Duffy provided access to FocusChat software (TNS Intersearch, Inc., formerly Greenfield Online) used for the online qualitative research in Appendix A. Bill MacElroy, Socratic Technologies, Inc., provided data from *Studies of Information, Research, and Consulting Services*, which were sponsored by the Institute for International Research and the Interactive Marketing Research Organization (IMRO). Data entry, proofreading, graphics, transcription, and electronic typesetting services were provided by associates of Research Publishers LLC. Included among the many who have helped are Karen Berendes, Teresa Cheng, Kristin Gill, Margaret A. Hogan, and Krista Sorenson. Special recognition is due to Dana H. James for copyediting, to Amy Hendrickson, TEXnology, Inc., for her assistance in the development of LaTeX class and style files, and to others within the TeX community for sharing software and services for electronic typesetting. Reviewers provided many helpful suggestions; included in this group are Neli Esipova, Mala Joshi, Nicholas H. Woolf, and Susan Yolton. And, of course, we thank family and friends who have supported us throughout the course of writing and editing.

Thomas W. Miller, Madison, Wisconsin
Jeff Walkowski, Minneapolis, Minnesota

January 20, 2004

Figures

Tables

Chapter 1

Varieties of Qualitative Research

Thomas W. Miller and Jeff Walkowski

The phone rings. A recruiter speaks: "I'm calling on behalf of the University of Wisconsin–Madison. We're studying student attitudes about careers. We're looking for students who are going to graduate this year. Are you a senior at the University?"

Chris says, "Yes."

"We'd like you to join a discussion group with five other seniors who will be talking about academic majors and careers. It should take less than ninety minutes, and you'll be paid twenty-five dollars for your time. It's voluntary. The information we collect will be kept confidential. Would you be interested in participating?"

Chris says she's interested and is told that the group will meet next Tuesday night at 7:00 P.M. "Are you free then?" the recruiter asks.

"Yes, that should work for me. Where do I go for the group?"

To her surprise, Chris learns that she doesn't meet with the group in person. This will be an online focus group. She can join the group by logging on to the World Wide Web from her personal computer at home or from one of the student computer labs on campus. Chris thinks, "Twenty-five dollars for ninety minutes on the Web—that's not bad." She gives the recruiter her e-mail address and gets a Web address and password for joining the group. On the day before the focus group, Chris receives telephone and e-mail messages reminding her about the group.

Tuesday night Chris uses her personal computer to connect to the focus group from home. She is one of six student participants who happens to arrive within minutes of one another. At first they find themselves in a virtual waiting room. There is informal conversation among the students before they are moved to a virtual focus group room.

The online focus group begins with instructions about how to use the software. A moderator explains the purpose of the research and guides the discussion, asking open-ended questions about the students' academic majors and career goals. Chris reads the discussion as it evolves. To say something to the group, Chris types into a text entry area below the running

> transcript and clicks on the "send" button. Her message appears within seconds for all to see. Moderator entries appear in boldface type; participant entries appear in normal type. The moderator and participants are identified by first names or pseudonyms. The moderator asks questions. Participants respond. There is interaction among participants. An electronic transcript, generated from everything that the moderator and participants type, is generated immediately at the end of the discussion.

The online focus group just described is an example of the methods we review in this book. This first chapter begins with a definition of qualitative research online. We review methods that rely upon specialized software for online focus groups, as well as methods that utilize general-purpose communications software. We provide a detailed discussion of online focus groups, and we introduce focused conversation, a method developed by the first author. In addition to the terms explained in this chapter, the glossary in Appendix D provides definitions of computer, communications, and qualitative research terms.

1.1 What Is Qualitative Research Online?

Traditional qualitative research comes in many varieties. Ethnographers are the prototypical observers, watching what people do in their natural and social environments: "What do people do at work and play? How do they live their lives? How do they organize themselves into groups? What is the meaning of culture?" Using in-depth interviews, phenomenologists probe the intricacies of human cognition: "How do people make sense out of what they see and hear? What do they believe? How do they view the world? What is the meaning of signs and symbols?" Research practitioners lead focus group discussions about topics of interest to their clients: "What does the voter think about the current candidates for governor? What would prompt the consumer to use these products and services? How does the viewer feel about the new TV commercial?"

A researcher's time is spent in what Miller (2000) has referred to as "the four Gs": generating, gathering, and grouping information, and then giving information to others. When we think of qualitative research online, we usually think about methods of data collection. Moderating online focus groups, interviewing, observing focused conversations or online behavior, searching text databases—these are methods for generating and gathering qualitative data.

What makes research qualitative? Qualitative data come to us unstructured, disorganized, free-form. We start with events as they occur, words as spoken, and we tell a story about them. It is not unusual, of course, for different researchers to tell different stories from the same data. But if we do our jobs right, if we are good researchers, we will stay close to the data, and our stories will ring true.

Qualitative research online can involve the analysis of secondary data, such as computer logs of user group discussions or e-mail communication. The qualitative researcher can conduct observational studies about human-computer interaction and online communication. Much online qualitative research is primary research,

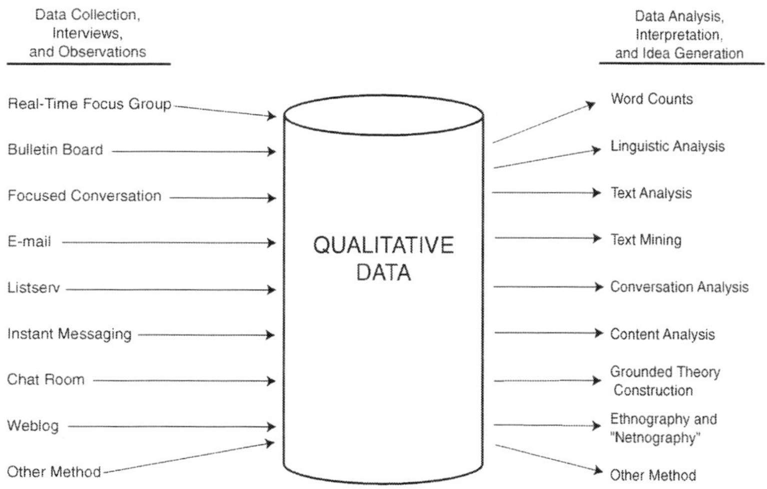

Figure 1.1: Qualitative Research Online: Methods of Data Collection and Analysis

involving customized studies designed for specific purposes, such as in-depth interviews and focus groups conducted online. Here is a general definition of qualitative research online:

> **Qualitative research online is qualitative research that relies upon networked computers as a vehicle for data collection.**

In recent years developed regions of the world have seen a rapid rise in Internet usage. In the United States, Canada, and Scandinavia there is widespread use of the Internet as a communication tool, with more than half of the adult populations having access to the Internet either at home or at work. People browse the Web, send e-mail messages to one another, use instant messaging, log on to message boards, and enter public and private chat rooms. As people become more comfortable with the Internet as a professional and personal communication medium, the Internet becomes a viable medium for business and social research.

Figure 1.1 provides an overview of qualitative research online. Online research applications for real-time and asynchronous focus groups and for focused conversations join other methods of online data collection, such as those based upon general-purpose communications software. These produce a wealth of qualitative data for analysis, interpretation, and theory generation. The analysis of online data proceeds in much the same way as the analysis of offline data. Accordingly, when we speak of "qualitative research online," we are usually referring to methods of data acquisition or data collection.

Providers and users of qualitative research online can acquire general-purpose software from public-domain or commercial sources. General-purpose software, including electronic mail (e-mail), listserv, instant messaging, chat room, and bulletin board software, may be used for primary or secondary research.

E-mail and Listservs

E-mail, a common store-and-forward communications tool, provides a convenient method for interpersonal communications. E-mail is asynchronous, meaning sender and receiver do not need to be online at the same time, and users do not need to be online to receive messages. To send or receive an e-mail message, the user establishes a connection to the network and executes the e-mail application. To send an e-mail message, the user must have the address of the intended recipient. To receive a message, the user runs the e-mail application, locates the message in an in-tray, and opens the message—like going to a mailbox, reaching in to get a letter, and opening the letter. Many e-mail facilities have utilities for notifying users that e-mail messages have been received. For those wishing to learn about how an electronic mail system is designed, Fuller (1983) provides a detailed discussion of the implementation of traditional e-mail store-and-forward messaging systems.

Listservs are utility programs for creating automated multi-user e-mail groups. User and special interest group messages sent to a listserv are automatically distributed to the e-mail addresses of list members. E-mail message logs from listservs provide rich sources of qualitative data because they are organized by user and special interest group topics.

Instant Messaging

Instant messaging, like e-mail, is an interpersonal communications tool. Senders and receivers of messages must have unique names or addresses. But instant messaging, as its name would imply, provides synchronous or real-time communications. It has the ability to detect the presence of other network users, people on a buddy list. Instant messaging sends messages only to those individuals who are connected to the network, running the instant messaging application, and on the buddy list. Instant messaging is a convenient method for hosting networked parties, conferences, or meetings among buddy-listed groups of friends or business associates. Instant messaging holds promise as a data collection method for qualitative research online.

At the present time, instant messaging lacks the extensive user base of e-mail. America Online (AOL) subscribers represent the largest segment of instant messaging users. Users of AOL instant messaging can send messages to other AOL users who happen to be online and on shared buddy lists for instant messaging. We expect future growth in instant messaging after protocol standards have been established and adopted by various Internet service providers (ISPs). Protocol standards make it possible to have multi-vendor interoperability. Kohda, Sugano, and Okuyama (2000) provide a review of instant messaging protocols and applications.

Chat Rooms and Bulletin Boards

The World Wide Web (WWW or Web), initially developed as a mechanism for hyperlinked document retrieval over the Internet, provides a facility for implementing additional general-purpose communication applications, including chat rooms and bulletin boards. These Web-browser-based applications require the user to log on by going to a World Wide Web address or Uniform Resource Locator (URL).

A chat room is a synchronous or real-time facility for communication within a group; it is an application running on a server on the Internet. To gain access to the application, chat room members type the URL for the chat room. After they enter the chat room, they are identified by their user names or by pseudonyms provided by the chat room administrator. Public chat rooms are open to all individuals with access to the Web. Organizations can use chat room software from public-domain or commercial sources to develop customized chat rooms for qualitative research. User names and passwords may be required to restrict access to certain individuals. It is also possible to provide individually coded URLs for selective entry into research chat rooms.

Bulletin boards, also called message boards or Web boards, are asynchronous facilities for communication among groups. Like chat rooms, these are application programs running on a server on the Internet. Access is via URLs, with public bulletin boards being open to anyone who has the URL. As with chat rooms, organizations can develop customized bulletin board applications using public domain or commercial software tools.

Unlike public chat rooms and bulletin boards, which are open to anyone with access to the Internet, most qualitative research online is designed for qualified respondents, members of target populations recruited for research purposes. Recruitment may be conducted by telephone, mail, e-mail, Web-based surveys, or a combination of modalities. Researchers give respondents personal identification numbers, passwords, and Web addresses for logging on to online research applications.

Much qualitative research online is also professionally moderated. Working from a discussion guide that has been prepared in advance and from an understanding of the information needs of research clients, a moderator keeps participants active, interested, and focused upon selected research topics. Detailed reviews of special-purpose applications are provided in subsequent sections of this chapter.

Weblogs

A Weblog or "blog" is a Web site with online information in a dated log format. Weblogs are useful for individuals and organizations wanting to provide current information relating to a particular content domain. Weblog postings may be viewed as personal statements or monologues, rather than online conversations.

As facilities for communities of users focused upon a common theme, posting information relevant to that theme, Weblogs represent rich sources of data for ethnographic analysis and qualitative research online.

Lindahl and Blount (2003) provide an overview of the history and technology of Weblogs, noting that they have grown in number from a handful in 1998 to more than a million in 2003. Weblog filters provide collections of URL links to other Web sites. Weblog journals provide personal diaries with dated entries, much like a bulletin board.

Weblog software simplifies the process of Web publishing for non-technical users. Weblogs can notify users of content updates. Weblogs can communicate with one another, offering a customized news service for users. Although much of the Weblog publication process is automated, an administrator can restrict user access to and manage content on a Weblog.

Internet Studies, Ethnography, and Online Communities

> In a culture like ours, long accustomed to splitting and dividing all things as a means of control, it is sometimes a bit of a shock to be reminded that, in operational and practical fact, the medium is the message. This is merely to say that the personal and social consequences of any medium—that is, of any extension of ourselves—result from the new scale that is introduced into our affairs by each extension of ourselves, or by any new technology.
>
> Marshall McLuhan *Understanding Media*, (1995)

The Internet is both an environment to be studied in its own right and a medium of research. It has been the subject of many studies of digital media and artistic expression (Holtzman 1994; Aarseth 1997; Bolter and Grusin 1999; Ryan 1999; Gauntlett 2000; Lunenfeld 2000; Scholder and Crandall 2001; Weibel and Druckrey 2001).

Traditional ethnography involves field observation, the study of social and consumer behavior in real life settings, as introduced by Wolcott (1994, 1999, 2001). Cell phones, including those with integrated cameras and personal data assistants, are changing the face of traditional ethnography. Traditional ethnography is becoming "digital ethnography," observation assisted by digital technology that may be easily transported into the field.

Online ethnography, virtual ethnography, or "netnography," as it has been called by Sherry and Kozinets (2001), concerns the study of online behavior itself. This is ethnographic research that draws upon computer- or network-based data and artifacts.

A burgeoning literature deals with online communication, culture, and social theory (Walther 1996; Davis and Brewer 1997; Jones 1997; Johnson 1997; Lévy 1997; Holeton 1998; Jones 1999; Jonscher 1999; Smith and Kollock 1999; Herman and Swiss 2000; Mann and Stewart 2000; Miller and Slater 2000; Huberman 2001; Lévy 2001). There are numerous studies of virtual communities or aggregations of individuals that emerge through communication over the Internet (Porter 1997;

Markham 1998; Cherny 1999; Smith and Kollock 1999; Rheingold 2000). Ellis, Oldridge, and Vasconcelos (2004) provide a useful review of this literature.

Generally speaking, an online community is a group of individuals that interacts online over an extended period of time. Large online communities, composed of thousands of participants, are possible. Werry and Mowbray (2001) provide numerous examples of large corporate-sponsored and nonprofit online communities. When used for primary research, online communities often consist of groups of fifty to two hundred people that have been recruited to participate in research about related topics over a period of three to twelve months.

Research with online communities may incorporate a variety of methods, including online surveys, real-time focus groups, and bulletin boards. Preece (2000), Powazak (2001), and McArthur and Bruza (2001) review critical success factors in developing online communities, including shared purpose, knowledge, and beliefs; participant commitment to repeated access over time; and technology for communication, shared resources, and data storage and retrieval.

Qualitative Data Analysis, Interpretation, and Theory Generation

The data of qualitative research online are words—text. A variety of methods have been suggested for the analysis of qualitative data. Linguists are interested in the text itself, in speech and communication patterns; their methods include linguistic, discourse, and conversation analysis. Social scientists and marketing researchers are interested in text as a way of understanding human experience (behavior, perceptions, opinions, and attitudes), using methods described as text, transcript, and content analysis.

Useful reviews of methods for qualitative data analysis and interpretation have been presented by others (Silverman 1993; Georgakopoulou and Goutsos 1997; Roberts 1997; Ryan and Bernard 2000; Silverman 2000a). Especially relevant to social scientists and marketing researchers is grounded theory construction (Glaser and Strauss 1967; Strauss and Corbin 1998; Dey 1999; Charmaz 2002).

Word counts, automated text summarization, and text data mining procedures search for regularities in word and phrase usage, turning words into numerical summaries. The distinction between qualitative and quantitative research becomes blurred when we work with various numerical approaches to qualitative data analysis. Reviews of content analysis methods have been presented by Schrott and Lanoue (1994), Silverman (2000b, 2001), and Neuendorf (2002). Computer-aided methods of text analysis have been discussed by others (Kelle 1995; Weitzman and Miles 1995; Roberts 1997; Stone 1997; Fielding and Lee 1998; Popping 2000; Weitzman 2000; West 2001; Seale 2002). Reviews of text mining may be found in Feldman (2002) and Miller (2005).

1.2 Online Focus Groups

Taking their name from traditional focus groups, online focus groups are group interviews guided by a moderator. In this section we identify two major types: synchronous (real-time) and asynchronous focus groups.

An online focus group is a moderated group interview conducted online either synchronously or asynchronously.

There are parallels between online and traditional face-to-face focus groups. In an online focus group, like a face-to-face group, there is a moderator, a group of participants, and observers. The observers are not visible to the participants. Participants are pre-qualified for the group to ensure that they have relevant demographics and experience for the group. The moderator is a trained discussion leader. The moderator begins the discussion by introducing himself or herself, explaining the purpose of the group, disclosing the fact that there are observers, and covering "ground rules" for all to follow. The discussion covers particular topic areas, agreed to in advance by the moderator and the research client. At the end of the online focus group, the moderator thanks participants for their time and opinions, and guides them out of the focus group.

There are differences between online and traditional focus groups. Face-to-face moderators often work from abbreviated discussion guides. Many moderator comments are extemporaneous and personal. When working online, the discussion guide is typically more explicit and complete. Things that might be said informally or extemporaneously in face-to-face communication should be formalized and typed out for an online group. Because the moderator isn't meeting with participants in person, the moderator may try to put his or her personality into the guide. The moderator's initial monologue, usually unwritten for face-to-face focus groups, needs to be part of the online discussion guide. As a result, online discussion guides are usually longer than face-to-face guides.

Face-to-face participants see name cards and faces around a table, whereas online participants see a computer screen with group members identified by their first names or pseudonyms. Face-to-face participants may be rewarded with good food, but they must travel to a common location to get the food. Online respondents often participate from their homes or workplaces. For face-to-face groups, moderators often show photographs, concept boards, videotapes, and other physical stimuli as part of the focus group. Online focus group applications provide virtual white boards for the display of digital stimulus materials, such as computer graphics and images.

Figure 1.2 provides a user's view of online focus group applications. There are the typical title, tool, and menu selections of a Microsoft Windows, Apple Macintosh, or Linux environment, maintained as they are when a Web browser is running. Typical browsers include Microsoft Internet Explorer, Netscape, Apple Safari, and Mozilla.

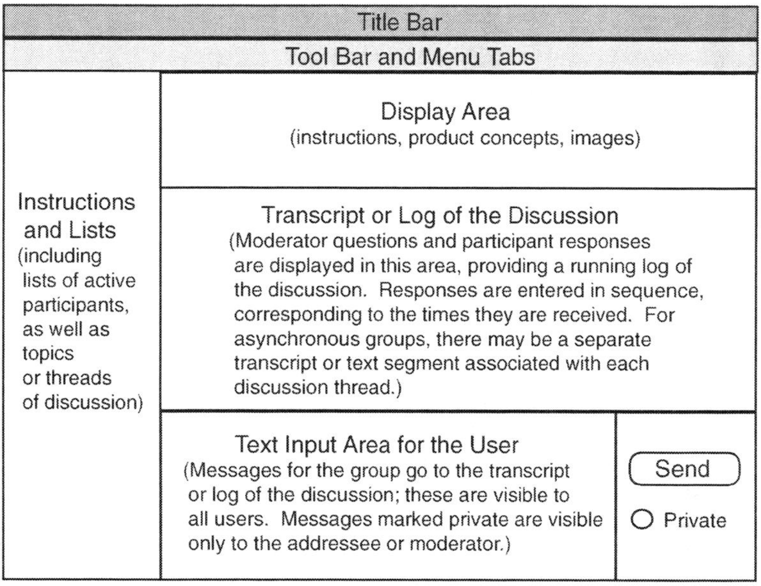

Figure 1.2: User's View of Qualitative Research Online

Figure 1.3 shows a generic information systems architecture for qualitative research online. Users, including moderators, participants, and observers on the client side, connect to a network through Web browsers. Conversational content is formatted, bundled in HTML tags, and communicated over the Internet using the HTTP protocol. Apache and Microsoft Web servers manage the interchange of dynamic conversational content across the Internet channel. Other information systems components include data collection applications, database services, and analytical services for text and data analysis.

To implement qualitative research online, systems programmers and administrators are responsible for system, network, and database management. The qualitative researcher (often the same person as the moderator) analyzes transcripts and data from online bulletin boards, synchronous focus groups, and surveys. Technical specialists sometimes work alongside of moderators, providing software and typing assistance with research applications. And there is the usual bevy of administrative support staff engaged in the recruitment and payment of focus group participants.

Real-Time Focus Groups

The real-time or synchronous focus group is a widely used online method. The real-time focus group is a guided group interview with all participants logged on

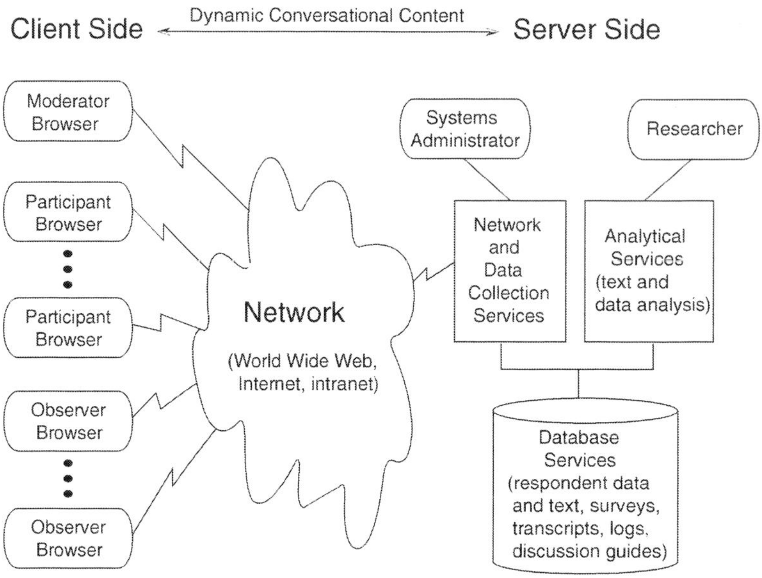

Figure 1.3: Information Systems Architecture for Qualitative Research Online

at the same time. It is common to have from six to twelve participants and a moderator involved in a real-time focus group.

Real-time focus groups are usually conducted with specialized software. Like chat room applications, real-time focus group applications permit users to connect to a synchronous online discussion using a standard Web browser. In addition to providing a facility for an online real-time discussion over the Internet, real-time focus group applications include special facilities for moderators and observers.

Figure 1.4 shows time lines for a real-time focus group, illustrating system availability, time online (connected), and time active (reading or typing messages) for three participants and a moderator. Participants, although online for most of the one- to two-hour focus group, are not equally active in their participation. Andy appears to be paying attention to something other than the focus group. Erika was online and active for most of the session, although she had a system failure preventing her from participating for a short period of time. Nicole had frequent interruptions and logged off early. Tyler, as we might hope for a moderator, was online and active for the entire period except for brief periods of inactivity or inattention.

System failures with real-time focus groups may result from computer or network problems. One participant having a system failure for a short period of time, as shown in the time lines for Erika, may be tolerated. Given the one- to two-hour duration of real-time focus groups, system failures of more than ten or

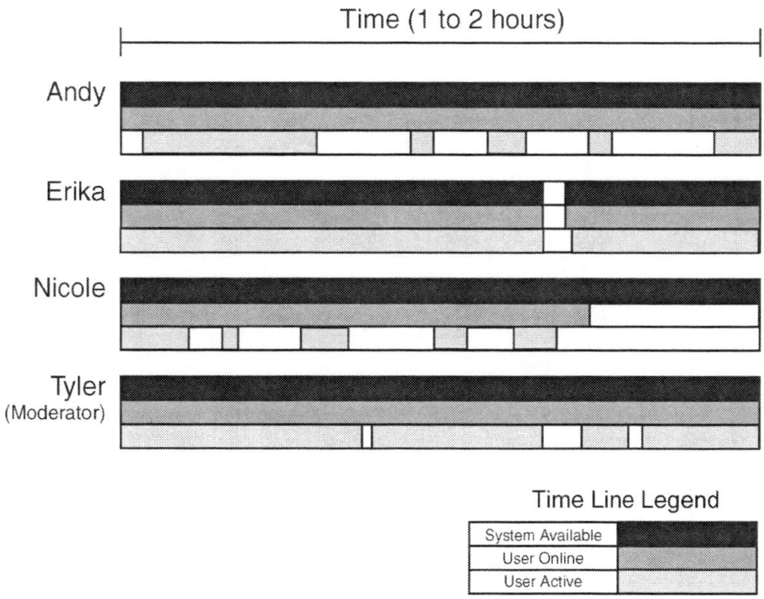

Figure 1.4: Participant and Moderator Time Lines for a Real-Time (Synchronous) Focus Group

fifteen minutes and system failures that affect all participants, such as server or network failures, can be very disruptive, affecting the flow of conversation. It is sometimes necessary to ignore data from groups run while experiencing system problems.

Current technology for real-time focus groups involves typing rather than talking. This makes the experience of the real-time focus group qualitatively different from that of a face-to-face group. For a face-to-face focus group, the moderator is likely to encourage participants to take turns, to speak one at a time. Not so with a real-time focus group. Online participants type responses simultaneously using their own computers. After responses are typed, participants send them to the discussion window, where they can be viewed by everyone. This simultaneity in response makes the discussion transcript appear disjointed or less like a sequential conversation. Because participants aren't taking turns in conversation, many discussion entries will appear to be out of order. Critics of real-time focus groups find this disconcerting.

Critics of real-time focus groups say the Internet is an alien environment in which to work and reliance upon typing hinders communication. The environment is impersonal, which keeps moderators from digging deeper into the real motivations and attitudes of respondents. Researchers may get short, top-of-mind responses rather than the rich responses they can get with face-to-face groups. With research participants working online, moderators can miss subtle cues in body language and tone of voice, which can be important in drawing valid inferences from the discussion.

Real-time focus group usage has grown despite the criticism. It has grown because well-designed software applications for online research have many advantages. In addition to utilizing the Internet with its worldwide reach, online focus groups offer opportunities for stimulus display, experimentation, and control not available with traditional focus groups. Because participants type their messages, a printed transcript of the discussion is easy to obtain.

From a moderator's point of view, the real-time focus group involves two concurrent discussions: (1) the focus group discussion among research participants and moderator, viewable by participants, moderator, and clients, and (2) the discussion among clients and moderator, viewable only by clients and moderator. Online focus group applications empower clients. Rather than having selected times for clients to send questions or suggestions to the moderator, as with a traditional face-to-face group, clients have continuous access to the moderator. They can ask questions, make suggestions, or send requests at any time without respondents knowing about these communications. If the moderator is willing to accommodate their requests, clients can have a substantial impact upon the direction of a focus group discussion.

Well-designed focus group applications also provide facilities for sending private messages to participants or clients. If a participant is dominating the discussion or making inappropriate remarks, the moderator can send a private message to encourage more cooperative and appropriate behavior. If the participant doesn't "shape up," the moderator can discretely drop the participant from the group. Private messages may also be sent to clients. Participants in the panel and bulletin board discussions of Chapters 2 and 3, respectively, provide additional thoughts about the advantages and disadvantages of real-time focus groups.

Bulletin Board Focus Groups

The bulletin board or asynchronous focus group has similarities to the real-time focus group. A moderator leads the discussion, using a guide prepared in advance. There is interaction among participants and probing from the moderator. Participants type their responses, which are visible to participants, clients, and the moderator. Because responses are typed, electronic transcripts are generated automatically by the software.

Asynchronous focus groups are usually conducted with specialized software. Like general-purpose bulletin board or message board applications, asynchronous focus group applications permit users to connect to an asynchronous discussion over the Internet using a standard Web browser. But, in addition to providing a facility for an online discussion, asynchronous focus group applications include special utilities for moderators and observers. Well-designed applications include facilities for private moderator-client and moderator-participant communications, as well as for the white board display of computer graphics and images.

The primary difference between a real-time group and an asynchronous group is its time frame for completion. While a real-time focus group takes an hour or two with moderator and participants logged on at the same time, an asynchronous focus group can take days or weeks to complete. Moderators and participants log on at different days and times. Another difference is the size of the group. While it is difficult to accommodate more than six to twelve real-time focus group respondents, asynchronous groups are often composed of groups of twelve to twenty, or even thirty respondents.

The moderator encourages asynchronous focus group participants to log on once or twice a day for the duration of the discussion. With each log-on, participants might be expected to spend fifteen to thirty minutes reading and responding to messages. Accordingly, the total time participants devote to the asynchronous focus group is likely to be greater than the time devoted to a real-time focus group.

Figure 1.5 shows an asynchronous focus group with system availability, time online (connected), and time active (reading or typing messages) for three participants and a moderator. Except for a short period of unavailability (perhaps due to a network or server failure), the focus group facility is available for days or weeks at a time. Participants log on for short periods of time and are active (reading and posting messages) for part of the time they are logged on. Individual system failures sometimes prevent a participant from being online, as shown in the time lines for Jon. System failures, even network or server failures of moderate length (an hour or two, say), may be tolerated in asynchronous focus groups because these focus groups are conducted over a period of days or weeks. Participant time lines are likely to show wide individual differences in online activity. We should expect time lines for the moderator to exhibit the highest frequency of log-ins and highest level of online activity.

The moderator of an asynchronous focus group is likely to log in two or more times a day, responding to participant messages and promoting involvement and interaction. The moderator also sends e-mail reminders to inactive participants, encouraging their involvement in the discussion. Accordingly, the total time a moderator devotes to an asynchronous focus group is likely to be greater than the time devoted to a real-time focus group.

Well-designed applications for asynchronous focus groups afford moderators an opportunity to post messages at predetermined times. We use the word "post" rather than "send" when talking about an asynchronous focus group because participants do not actually see moderator messages until they log on to the focus group and request to see them. To accompany the discussion guide, software for asynchronous focus groups provides a schedule for the posting of moderator messages and white board stimuli.

Asynchronous focus groups have an epistolary quality. The moderator sends a message, beginning a sequence of related statements or discussion thread. Time passes, and participants post their replies. Time passes, more replies are posted.

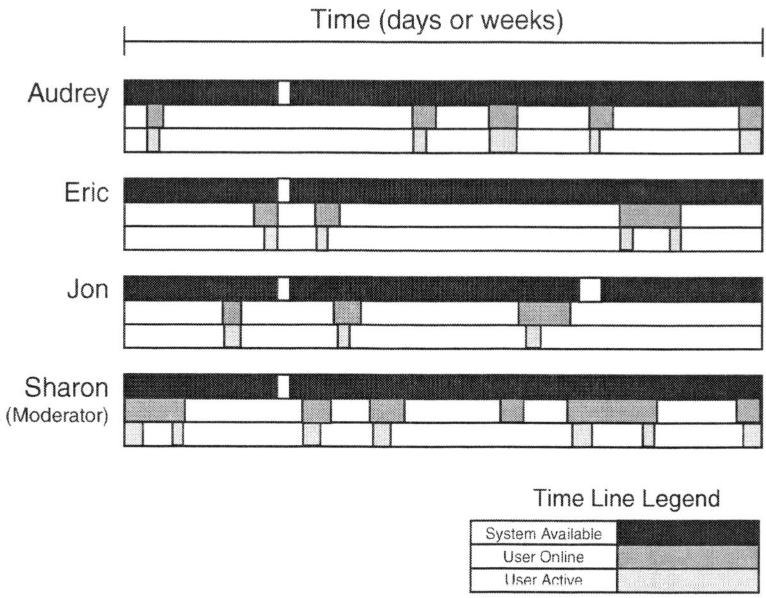

Figure 1.5: Participant and Moderator Time Lines for a Bulletin Board (Asynchronous Focus Group)

Time passes, and the moderator sends another message, beginning a second discussion thread. Like letters between distant friends or lovers, accumulated over time and saved for future reading, the transcript for an asynchronous focus group becomes the record of a virtual relationship, a meeting of minds or sharing of opinions over time.

Because participants can join in or continue with the discussion at any place or time, a mechanism is needed for providing order to the discussion. What provides order in an asynchronous focus group discussion is its organization along discussion threads. Each new message from the moderator begins a new discussion thread. Discussion threads remain active for the duration of the asynchronous focus group. Relying, as we often do, upon the intelligence and goodwill of participants, we hope that messages falling under a discussion thread are indeed relevant to that thread.

Asynchronous focus groups share many of the advantages and disadvantages of real-time focus groups and online research in general. In addition, asynchronous focus groups have special value for working with professional or hard-to-reach participant groups. Busy people find it hard to attend real-time focus groups, which require all participants to be logged on concurrently. An asynchronous focus group gives participants the opportunity to log on at various times during the day or night, weekday or weekend, for the duration of the study.

Asynchronous focus groups are also good for discussions of difficult, thought-provoking topics. Because they occur over a period of days or weeks, participants don't feel rushed and don't need to wait for others to type their responses. Asynchronous focus groups give participants time to describe not just what they think, but also how they came to their conclusions. Lengthy, in-depth responses are common as people discuss their reasoning. The discussion in Chapter 3 shows participants sharing thoughts with one another in an asynchronous focus group conducted especially for this book.

1.3 Focused Conversation

Moderators and research clients want to hear about discussion topics in the participants' words. The objective is to get respondents to talk freely without making assumptions about their understanding of topics and without introducing concepts or words that reflect the biases of the moderator or client.

Focus group moderators strive to intervene as little as possible in focus group conversations. They try to ask the one "magic" question that will allow a group of participants (a dyad or triad perhaps) to continue with its own lengthy conversation, hitting important topics of discussion. Moderators in training are encouraged to strive for "rolls," times in the discussion when a group is, without knowing it, self-moderating. These are the times when entire pages of a transcript show no moderator interruptions.

A moderator might say, "Imagine that I'm a fly on the wall, just listening in. Talk with each other, not to me. But, like a fly, I might occasionally 'land' on the table, ask a question, or steer your group in a direction it needs to go. Remember, you are the center of attention, not me."

Despite the best of intentions, good moderators will never be "flies on the wall." They are not invisible, not so long as they are in the room or identified by name on the computer screen. Experimenter effects are alive and well in qualitative research, with participants trying to please moderators, interviewers, and observers. Is there a way to have a more natural conversation among participants, an unmoderated conversation?

Online conversations without moderators are commonplace. They may be observed in e-mail and instant messages between friends and acquaintances. They are seen in public chat rooms, listservs, and bulletin boards. People talk with people, sharing opinions and information about many topics of interest to social and business researchers. What these free-flowing conversations lack is structure and focus, qualities that can be provided by a conversation guide.

Although the term "focused conversation" could easily be used to describe many qualitative research methods, including in-depth interviews and moderated focus groups, in this book we use the term to describe online conversations without an interviewer or moderator interacting with participants. A focused conversation is an open-ended conversation among research participants with the focus provided by a conversation guide. Because there is no interviewer or moderator guiding the conversation, the focused conversation is participant self-directed or self-moderated.

Focused conversation is qualitative research online with a small self-moderating group and a conversation guide to provide focus.

A focused conversation is first and foremost a conversation. The objective is to learn about people in their own words. In his book on interviewing, Kvale (1996) argued for the primacy of conversation in qualitative research. In his words, "Conversation is a basic mode of human interaction. Human beings talk with each other—they interact, pose questions, and answer questions. Through conversations we get to know people, get to learn about their experiences, feelings, and hopes" (Kvale 1996, p. 5).

Imagine a focused conversation between two people, much like a series of letters or messages being exchanged over time. The time frame could be short (twenty to sixty minutes for a real-time focus group) or long (days or weeks for an asynchronous focus group). What matters is not the time, but the depth of conversation, the extent to which participants challenge one another to explain their points of view.

A focused conversation between two people is like an in-depth, open-ended interview without the interviewer. We can think of it as concurrent individual interviews with peers taking turns as interviewer and interviewee. What we hope to achieve from focused conversation is a medium in which participants freely pose and respond to questions in their own words. There will be interaction among participants, but that interaction is not directly influenced by a moderator.

To have a focused conversation, the researcher prepares a conversation guide, consisting of stimulus events and a schedule for their presentation. Stimulus events include participant instructions, questions for discussion, and materials for review. Stimulus events may be set to occur at pre-specified times or triggered by participant requests or conversation conditions, such as the number of words typed in response to a prior question, the number of messages sent by participants, or observed lulls in real-time conversation.

Online technology helps to implement the focused conversation. E-mail, instant messaging, chat, or online focus group software could be used. Asynchronous focus group applications may be used, given their capability for organizing discussion along threads and posting text messages and white board stimulus materials at designated times. Still better is specialized software designed for focused conversation.

In a focused conversation, research participants read from the conversation guide and type their responses. They have conversations with one another about the topics listed in the guide. As with online focus groups, participants' typed responses are collected and stored by the software application, producing an automatic transcript of the conversation. But unlike online focus groups, there is no moderator for the conversation itself.

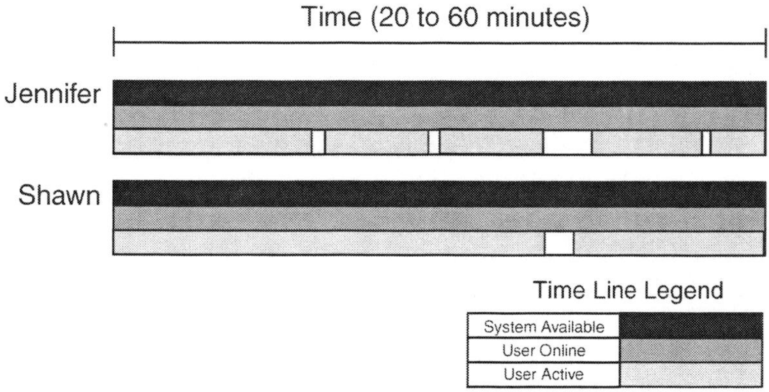

Figure 1.6: Participant Time Lines for a Synchronous Focused Conversation

A focused conversation between two people is likely to show explicit turn-taking. There is the natural reciprocity of a two-person dialogue. With each new discussion topic, there is an initial opportunity for participants to respond simultaneously. But as the discussion continues, turn-taking emerges. Suppose Jennifer and Shawn respond to a question from a conversation guide. Jennifer reads Shawn's response and sends her reply. Shawn replies to Jennifer's message. Jennifer replies to Shawn's message, and so on, until Jennifer and Shawn address the next topic of conversation from the guide. Turn-taking in focused conversation results in a transcript that reads like a natural conversation. There is sequence; there is flow.

Figure 1.6 shows time lines for a synchronous focused conversation, such as one that might be conducted using a real-time focus group application, chat room, or instant messaging software. With a synchronous focused conversation of twenty to sixty minutes, we should expect participants to be online and active most of the time. Periods of inactivity are sometimes coordinated, with participants agreeing to take short breaks at the same time, as shown for Jennifer and Shawn. Figure 1.7 shows time lines for an asynchronous focused conversation, such as one that might be conducted using asynchronous focus group, e-mail, or bulletin board software.

Participants in asynchronous focused conversations can coordinate schedules, sharing their plans for online activity over the days or weeks of a study. There may be times when participants are online at the same time, experiencing the immediacy of a synchronous conversation. Chapter 4 shows the transcript of an asynchronous focused conversation between the authors of this book. Before the conversation began the authors agreed to log on twice a day, once in the morning and once in the afternoon or evening. Hy Mariampolski, an expert in qualitative market research, offered questions for the conversation guide but did not interact with the focused conversation.

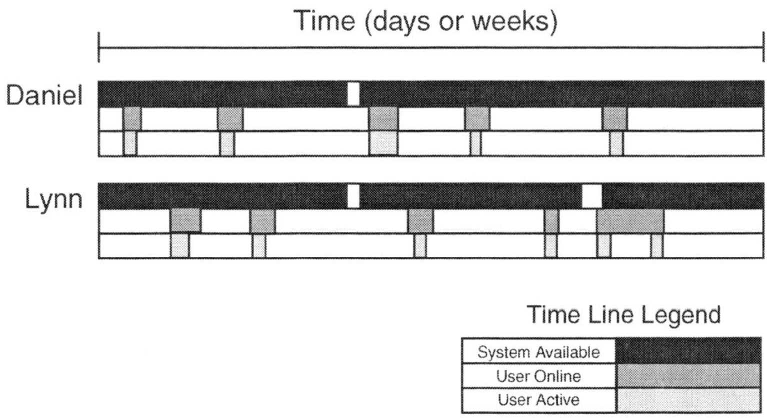

Figure 1.7: Participant Time Lines for an Asynchronous Focused Conversation

1.4 A Classification of Methods

We can provide a general classification of methods for qualitative research online by noting (1) whether or not a researcher, interviewer, or moderator is actively involved with participants and (2) the synchronous or asynchronous time frame for the research. As shown in Figure 1.8, special-purpose and general-purpose software may be placed within such a classification scheme.

An interview involves an interviewer (moderator) and one or more interviewees (participants). Online focus groups, reviewed in previous sections, are group online interviews. It is also possible to conduct online individual interviews or what are often called "one-on-ones." The interviewer leads an interviewee in a conversation related to research topics of interest. Online individual interviews can make use of specialized software for online focus groups or general-purpose software for e-mail, instant messaging, listservs, chat rooms, and bulletin boards. The online interview, whether synchronous or asynchronous, usually takes place over the Internet.

Interviews put the researcher (interviewer, moderator) in direct contact with research subjects (respondents, participants). The researcher is active, asking questions, listening, and probing. Synchronous interviews and conversations take place in real time with fully overlapping time intervals for moderators and participants. Asynchronous interviews and conversations take place across the same period of time, but do not require overlapping time intervals for moderators or participants. Mann and Stewart (2002) provide a review of online interviewing.

Traditional field observation has its online analogue in online observation. Online observation is conducted by observing the behavior of computer and network users as it happens. More common is observation of online behavior after it happens, which is a form of database research. Databases include computer records of

Do researcher and subjects interact?

Time Lines	*Yes (Interview)*	*No (Observation)*
Synchronous	Real-time Focus Group Instant Messaging Chat Room	Focused Conversation Instant Messaging Chat Room
Asynchronous	Bulletin Board E-mail Listserv	Focused Conversation E-mail, Listserv Bulletin Board Weblog Online Survey (open-ended questions)

Figure 1.8: From Interview to Observation: A Classification of Methods for Qualitative Research Online

past organizational behavior and text documents relevant to the purposes of qualitative research. These data, collected as part of the day-to-day communication activities of organizations, arise from synchronous applications like instant messaging and chat, and asynchronous applications like e-mail, listservs, and bulletin boards.

Focused conversations and observational studies do not put the researcher in direct contact with research subjects. Open-ended text responses from online surveys provide an additional data source for qualitative research online. Like focused conversations and observational studies, these do not put the researcher in direct contact with subjects.

1.5 Researcher Responsibilities

Methods of qualitative research online offer great promise as technologies for learning about people. But having the ability to collect and analyze data quickly and thoroughly does not excuse researchers from their obligation to conduct research in a responsible manner, recruiting with research participant opt-in and opt-out, protecting people's confidentiality, and being respectful of people's time.

Online researchers must be ever vigilant in respecting the privacy of research participants. Professional organizations of researchers, such as the American Marketing Association (AMA), the Council of American Survey Research Organizations (CASRO), the Qualitative Research Consultants Association (QRCA), and the World Association of Research Professionals (ESOMAR), publish codes of conduct for their members. The Interactive Marketing Research Organization (IMRO) provides a code of ethics for conducting online research, which is reproduced in Appendix B. Additional discussion of confidentiality, privacy, and online research ethics may be found in Sharf (1999), Bakardjieva and Feenberg (2001), Miller and James (2003), and a special issue of *The Information Society Journal* (1996, vol. 12, no. 2).

Copyright of intellectual property is another area of importance to qualitative research online. Technology gives us the ability to construct massive document collections of text through Web searches and downloads. But serious questions emerge concerning the appropriate use of document collections. Borrull and Oppenheim (2004) review legal issues relating to data collected from the World Wide Web.

Government publications and factual information cannot be copyrighted, but most other information on the World Wide Web is protected by copyright. The fact that developers and authors can distribute their works freely across the Web, placing content in the public domain while retaining copyright, introduces difficulties for consumers and users of these works. Qualitative researchers, using results from Web searches, such as published documents from chats, bulletin boards, and Weblogs, need to respect authors' copyright.

Chapter 2

Applications of Online Research

Qualitative research online was the topic of a panel discussion at the 2000 EXPLOR Forum in Chicago. Rather than narrating a panel in the typical conference format, author Jeff Walkowski moderated the qualitative research panel as though it were a focus group. Views from the field can be heard from expert practitioners interacting with one another. Although conducted in November 2000, their discussion is as relevant today as it was then. We provide the edited transcript from that discussion in this chapter. The transcript identifies participants by last name, and Appendix C gives biographies of the panelists.

2.1 Prologue

Before viewing the transcript from the panel discussion, we note that there is widespread agreement among panelists that online qualitative methods offer numerous advantages over more traditional forms of qualitative research. Included among these advantages are:

- Online qualitative research offers anonymity for respondents, which can be highly desirable when dealing with sensitive issues.
- Usability studies of Web sites and Web-based material are enhanced when users are in their own environment (home or office) using their own PC, monitor, and chosen Web browser. Online qualitative allows this form of usability study.
- When the incidence of a participant characteristic is low, making it unfeasible to recruit a group in a given geographical market, online qualitative research allows the researcher to recruit from a wider geographical area.
- When relevant geographic markets are global in scope and budget constraints prohibit travel to all desired markets, online qualitative research permits all to be included in the sample pool. Furthermore, the message board option provides flexible and equal access to respondents across time zones.

Some panelists suggest that online qualitative methods broaden the potential use of qualitative research, rather than drawing researchers away from traditional qualitative methods. Panelists review myths and realities concerning qualitative research online:

- Myth: Online focus groups will replace traditional focus groups.

  Reality: Proponents of online research, such as the members of this panel, continue to use and embrace traditional methods.

- Myth: Respondents do not interact with each other in online focus groups.

  Reality: Online respondents do interact with one another. Online moderators report instances in which it is difficult to adjourn online groups because participants have bonded with one another. Transcripts from bulletin board groups often include lengthy conversations among participants.

- Myth: Online qualitative research is less expensive than traditional (in-person or phone) research methods.

  Reality: There is an obvious savings in travel and facility rentals, but recruitment, incentives, and analysis costs are comparable to traditional forms of qualitative research.

- Myth: Online qualitative research is faster than traditional (in-person or phone) qualitative research methods.

  Reality: In some instances (e.g., when the issues are straightforward and the target audience is easy to define and recruit), online qualitative may be faster; however, the time needed for careful upfront planning could make an online project take just as long to complete as a traditional project.

Panelists recognize several barriers limiting the adoption of online qualitative methods. Some researchers believe that without the ability to see respondents' body language and hear their voice inflections, researchers are missing out on too much information to make online approaches useful. Some researchers fear that proprietary information (e.g., ideas, concepts, images of product prototypes) presented in online focus sessions are more likely to be captured and leaked outside the group. Researchers may feel handicapped in that they cannot use all of the interventions in online groups that they are accustomed to using in traditional settings, such as product sorts, teamwork exercises, and building collages.

While panelists are unaware of how much qualitative research is conducted online, panelists agree that online qualitative expenditures represent less than 5 percent of the total qualitative research expenditures. Still, panelists are satisfied with the technique, finding new uses for it and speaking with zeal about the approach. They anticipate adoption rates to grow, although possibly less quickly than they may wish.

2.2 Snapshot: Online Qualitative Today

WALKOWSKI Okay, what I'd like to do is start off with an overview, a snapshot. Where do you see things going today in terms of trends in online qualitative? Talk a little about your impressions of the market's receptivity to online qualitative. Anybody?

KINDIG Okay, I will start. I'm going to speak specifically from the pharmaceutical perspective in my current role, though I have also worked as a generalist at another firm covering many different industries. And I would say that some of these trends are the same. In pharmaceutical research, though, I would say that market receptivity is fairly scattered and fragmented. It seems to hinge strongly upon the corporate culture of the business. I would say (not surprisingly) those firms that have embraced advances in business technology and have made resource commitments to adoption and development of technology are those who are more open to all types of innovative, qualitative research. That could be online data collection, online real-time transmission of data, multimedia reporting, et cetera. And those firms which have not made that type of commitment are less open to the idea of online research. That said, because client openness to technology is not something over which we have a tremendous amount of control as researchers, I do see another factor that appears to impact interest among those companies that are more likely to try online qualitative, and that is the investment that the researcher or research firm has made in client education. That could be through giving demonstrations or learning sessions to clients, offering a blend of online and traditional research on an initial project to bring someone to the world of online qualitative, providing interactive proposals with embedded demonstrations to clients, or sharing examples of nonproprietary research.

KLUG I'll make a couple of comments here. I think as people have adapted to Internet research, one of the low-hanging fruits is to grasp the idea of taking qualitative research and adapting it to the Internet. It's not quite so crystal clear as to how you take a focus group and adapt it to an online environment. In fact, we probably do ourselves a bit of a disservice by labeling some of our chat sessions "focus groups" or "online focus groups" when in reality we need a new terminology for them. It's really a new methodology, and it should not be confused with face-to-face focus groups.

ROTH I would just like to add to that. A lot of the work that we do online is also done in traditional groups, like concept tests and positioning studies, and that's a pretty easy transition. But there are groups or sessions that we do on online bulletin boards that allow clients to do work that they couldn't have done otherwise.

WALKOWSKI Does anybody have any numbers that they could share in terms of where online qualitative is going? Has it been stable over the

past couple of years? Is it going up, is it going down? Anybody have any clues about that?

WEBER We've noticed a slow and steady increase in usage of our online focus group facility partly because more people are coming online and doing it. Market researchers like to step back and take a look at new technology before they accept it. Now that we have gotten past some of the technology barriers that we were initially faced with, integration of online with traditional methods is going to happen.

WALKOWSKI Anybody else have any evidence one way or the other?

KLUG Just from our experience we saw a real spike. We started doing these things three years ago. We saw it really spike up the second year. And now it seems to have flattened out. We've had a bulletin board discussion group product in place, and its acceptance is slow. But people who do use it seem to enjoy it; they get good information from it. But again, I wouldn't call it the high-rise growth element of our interactive business.

ROTH For the past four years, the amount of online qualitative at Greenfield has grown about 300 percent a year, but I'd also say there's a leveling out of that. That leveling out could be due to market conditions. But also, as more and more companies get into it, I think that they are demanding services to be faster and closer to what they're used to from traditional research, even though there are differences in the methodology. I don't think that online and traditional should be compared head-to-head.

WALKOWSKI How about the use of real-time chats versus message boards? Bernie [Klug], you just talked about having a message board or bulletin board. I know that Greenfield has them, and I know Itracks has them. Can you give us any indication or projections about where you see that going? How does that balance out—chats versus message boards? Where is it headed and why?

KLUG Good question. I think that, at least in the work we do, these tools are nice-to-have tools. And they're not part of the mainstream qualitative research work that our clients typically do. The discussion group is where the real application seems to lie. We find that for an audience for a particular behavior, denture wearers, say, you'd like to have a group of forty to fifty denture wearers to whom you could pose an open-ended question and from whom you could get a reaction in twenty-four or thirty hours. And you can have those people available to you for an extended length of time. And as we pose questions, an e-mail message is automatically sent out. You probably know how the method works. And it can be a very informative way to get some quick insight into an idea that you might come up with on your drive into work or riding on the train. And I see that as where one of the values lies. In a more structured environment, we haven't seen quite so much application in our experience.

WALKOWSKI **So it sounds like you're saying—correct me if I'm wrong—that you see more value in the message board types of research than real-time.**

KLUG Oh no, not necessarily, it's just a difference of application. Understand what you're trying to accomplish, and then use the right tool for that particular application.

WALKOWSKI **Other thoughts?**

WEBER We find that, when there are specific groups of professionals, like doctors, researchers tend to choose a bulletin board over a focus group in real time.

WALKOWSKI **Why is that?**

WEBER I think in some cases there may be difficulty getting these people together at a time that's appropriate for everyone. And, perhaps, there is a need for more in-depth answers, which you can't get when you're working with an hour and a half. With the bulletin board, professional people have as much time as possible to complete their answers.

KINDIG I would say that our experience is similar. Our growth is in the area of bulletin boards. Again, I make the caveat that that's predominantly with people in the pharmaceutical and biotech area; so it's a lot of physicians in managed care organizations. I would agree with Dan [Weber] that bulletin boards are appealing to these types of professionals. I actually think that it has to do with the depth of information that's gathered. Sometimes the information that we gather in the course of a week could be published as white papers. People are spending a tremendous amount of time, their personal time, to respond. But also, I think there is sort of an ego appeal in being asked to be part of a panel of experts to talk about an issue that fits more with someone's self-perception about the type of research in which they would want to participate. I would agree that it is not a better-versus-worse comparison between the two types of methodologies, just as it's not a better-versus-worse comparison between online and offline. I know that we've developed a series of decision trees that we go through with our clients in order to determine which might be the appropriate methodology (whether it's online or offline) and arrive at the best methodologies through that.

WEBER I think one of the key points is how quickly the clients want the results. Obviously, when somebody comes to us and says, "We need this right now." Well, if you need it right now, we're not going to do a two-week bulletin board.

WALKOWSKI **Can you talk a little bit about how you know what share of the clients are coming to you and asking for the quick results with real-time chats versus having the luxury of some time with message board discussions?**

WEBER Right now, the majority of our groups are the real-time focus groups. But we're seeing a rapid growth in the bulletin boards as well; so I would say it's about four to one online focus groups over bulletin boards right now.

ROTH We are doing probably a similar percentage breakdown in focus groups versus bulletin boards, and I think that's due to the fact that online focus groups have been around now long enough that people understand what they are. And we have found that, as clients explain their objectives to us and we present the concept of online bulletin boards (if that's the appropriate methodology), there's great acceptance of bulletin boards at that point.

WALKOWSKI One more question on current trends before we move on to the next topic. What about the projects that you are involved in? Do they tend to be exclusively online? To what extent are there qualitative projects that mix both traditional and online methods?

ROTH I'll explain quickly. We only do online work, but we often work with clients who are doing traditional and online research.

KINDIG Sometimes it depends on the research objective. As has been stated before, regarding online quantitative projects, there are opportunities to do qualitative research that, perhaps, could not have been done before if we weren't using online methods. So in that case it's purely online research that we do. Though, as I mentioned previously, sometimes there's an opportunity (if it's possible to combine traditional and online) to ease people into online research who may be concerned about its effectiveness by doing "quasi-parallel" studies with both online and offline. So we do some of that.

2.3 Online vs. Offline: Is One Better?

WALKOWSKI Okay, let's move on. We are constantly hearing about "better, faster, cheaper" in association with online research. But what I'd like to focus on is the "better." Is online qualitative ever better than face-to-face or traditional telephone qualitative? If so, when and in what cases?

ESIPOVA There are several situations where online is better. First of all, as was mentioned, online may be better than traditional when you need to do the research very quickly. Another time when online may be better is when you have to talk about sensitive issues. People might be more comfortable with online. Online may be better for getting to hard-to-reach people, doctors, lawyers. Some clients who want to do online research have offices around the country. They want to bring people from different locations to one focus group. But for me the main advantage of an online focus group is the fact that there is no leader in the group. Because everybody types at the same time, the discussion starts only after everybody gives a first opinion.

WEBER In a classic example, we do a lot of beta testing of e-commerce sites. Clients want to create the environment with a person at home, going through a purchasing process and giving feedback on it. I think there's no better way to do that than online as opposed to traditional. There are certain applications where it just makes sense.

ROTH I'd also add that in the case of concept tests, we have found that respondents are very forthright online. They will say things in an online group that they wouldn't say in a traditional group, especially when they dislike a concept.

WALKOWSKI I've heard that before, and I have that same feeling when I do online groups. But I don't have any proof of that—I just have a gut feeling—it's a qualitative assessment. I'm wondering, have you gone any further than I have in trying to document or demonstrate that?

ROTH Well, I can't say that I've documented it, but I can tell you that clients have corroborated that that is the case. They might have walked away from the traditional group having a mixed feeling about respondent feedback that they got. When they come out of an online group, they're much more sure about respondent feedback. The other area in which I think online groups are better is with low-incidence groups. Again, we are simply doing projects that wouldn't have been done otherwise. Some people can't get to a traditional focus group facility because they're so remote or because they're disabled in some way.

KINDIG Online focus groups are also wonderful for promoting innovation in design. We've been able to do some groups that we wouldn't have been able to do traditionally, such as mixing physicians and patients in the same group and getting very interesting and different kinds of feedback than if you were to conduct separate patient and physician groups. So you can bring innovation to the work that you do.

WALKOWSKI Let me ask about that. I don't do medical research. Why couldn't you mix patients and physicians in the same room?

ROTH The patient's opinion often gets suppressed when you mix doctors and patients together. (Forgive me if these are all health care examples, but I'm sure that you can think of examples that are applicable to your companies.) For many health issues it is very useful to divide groups along gender; so that you only have groups with women or groups with men. With online groups you can mix groups gender-wise because people's identities are protected. And if their handles, tag lines, or names on the computer screen are generic, you can't tell if it's a man or a woman who is typing. That sometimes leads to very interesting dynamics in a group that you couldn't achieve in a face-to-face group.

WALKOWSKI So what is it about online that permits us to mix patients and doctors or to do groups that we wouldn't normally do face-to-face?

KLUG I think it's that sense of anonymity. You're a tag line in a chat room. You might be identified as a particular profession or as having a particular behavior, but you're still anonymous. You can hide behind that tag line and be as honest as you want. Another advantage of online is its worldwide scope. (We just did this earlier this week.) We conducted a worldwide focus group that crossed respondents in the United Kingdom, United States, and Australia. We conducted the group Monday morning here; I guess it was about 11:00 A.M. We got U.K. people at 5:00 P.M. their time, and it was the next day in Australia. That would be a pretty tough thing to do with a regular focus group. So there are things that you can do with the power of the Web that we can't really think about doing with traditional methods.

WALKOWSKI Let me go back to a point somebody made yesterday at the EXPLOR Forum. (And I'm playing devil's advocate here.) Somebody said, "Just because we can do it, doesn't mean we should." So in the case of doing groups with an international audience just because we can, does that mean we should?

KINDIG I'll give you an example. I'm doing a global study right now. It's in the English language. It's a bulletin board study with opinion leaders in a very specific medical therapeutic area. I want to talk across several countries to the leading physicians and researchers in this therapeutic area. They are brought together in an expert forum in a bulletin board format. That is an extremely appropriate application of global online research.

WEBER I think the one other area would be very sensitive issues. When you're dealing with sensitive topics, people feel they can speak out from the comfort of their own home.

WALKOWSKI I would like to touch on the anonymity argument. I've heard the argument made on both sides. One is that because it's anonymous, people have no reason to hide their true feelings. They'll share ideas. And, based on what you said, it sounds like that's what you're experiencing. But I've heard the other side of the argument; that because it is anonymous, people can actually take on a different personality or a different persona and for the fun of it give us untruthful responses. I'd like some comments on that, please.

ROTH I'm sure that's possible. I don't see any incentive for them to do that. And it's certainly possible for them to do that in traditional groups as well.

KLUG One of the things about these tools is that the moderator has, let's say, quick and powerful capabilities. If you do sense that someone is "pulling your chain" or really being disruptive, with a click that guy is gone. And in a real environment, of course, that isn't quite so convenient, unless maybe we've got someone big standing beside the moderator to muscle the guy out of the room. But still, that would certainly be disruptive.

ROTH Yes, I just want to add that, as in the case with traditional groups, it really is moderator skill that comes into play, gently challenging the person to back up his or her answers. I don't think that many moderators would let the situation get out of control.

2.4 Recruitment Issues

WALKOWSKI Okay, let's move on to another topic and that is recruitment. What recruitment methods work best for online qualitative and why?

WEBER We work with many companies. Some use interactive panels; others recruit by telephone. There's a wide mix. It comes back to the type of research that you're doing and what is most appropriate. There's still some element of human contact that's required to bring people to the groups. We've found that if a telephone call is made to the people the day of the focus group, informing them or reminding them to take part in the group, then the show-up rate is significantly increased. Yes, there is something personal taking place here. Although it's not a physical type of environment, there is something about the human contact that's important to getting people to show up.

ESIPOVA I agree with that. It's very important to use e-mail lists from your clients or some list you have already. When you need people to participate, it is best to call shortly before the group is supposed to meet.

KINDIG We also use the phone as our primary means. (I should say, it depends on the sample. Sometimes you receive an e-mail sample, and that's your initial means of contacting potential respondents if you're recruiting from a known community of users or something like that.) We actually rely on a minimum of two phone contacts in addition to our providing the respondents with registration information by e-mail. We use the phone first to screen the respondents to have a live voice, making sure that this is actually the kind of person that we want to talk to. And also, as you are saying, to "up the ante" in terms of people showing up. And then we use a phone call the day of the group. We used to have a 25 percent show rate, and now that is up to about a 60 percent show rate if we use day-of phone calls. Online focus groups still have lower participation rates than face-to-face groups, but a phone call significantly increases participation rates.

KLUG We use primarily e-mail methodologies to find our participants. And of course, we're recruiting them from our interactive panel of participants. And that e-mail is going to look for the purchase behavior (whatever it is that we're looking for) to make sure we've got the right audience. And then, in addition to that, we'll do a little screening about their computer environment, their access to the Web, making sure that they've got the right (compatible) browser and things of that sort. Now, that's getting to be less of a problem than it was a few years ago. But you still want to make sure that you don't get somebody into the group that has a 14.4 kilobits per second modem when you're putting up a megabyte's worth of full-motion video or something, because they're just not going to be able to participate. Then we contact participants within twenty-four hours before the session is to occur with another e-mail. And we make available an 800 number that they can call to ensure that they're able to get into the group. We've got their phone number; so we can call them to see if they're having trouble. You have to do the same thing for your observer group as well because observers are not always going to be able to get to the site, get logged in, and get into the online observation room as readily as you would think. You need to be able to support them; so you can hand-hold them through the process a few minutes before the session begins.

ESIPOVA I would like to add one more thing. We did a study with the A. C. Nielsen Center for Marketing Research comparing focus groups in different modalities: face-to-face, online, and telephone. And one of our observations was that, to have the same number of participants in focus groups across modalities, you have to put more effort into recruitment for the online groups. There was about a 10 percent difference in show-up rates between face-to-face and online groups. When you call to ask people to participate, the rates of agreeing to participate are the same. But when the participants actually have to come to the focus groups, rates for online groups are lower than for face-to-face groups.

ROTH We recruit primarily by e-mail from our database. We screen online; we rescreen online. People have to answer the screening questions the same way each time. And in the case of recruiting from a client list, we will have the client send an e-mail invitation [to potential recruits] to take a screener, and we'll take it from there. Again, we screen and rescreen online groups.

WALKOWSKI Bernie [Klug] and Susan [Roth], it sounds like you both primarily use the Internet for the recruitment and the reminder contacts for online groups. Can you tell us what kind of show rates you get in your groups? I'm sure it varies by industry, but can you give us a feeling?

KLUG We usually try to get eight to ten people in a group, and we'll recruit about twelve to fourteen to get that number.

ROTH We're aiming at six to eight to participate, and we recruit thirteen. We usually get ten who show. Somebody at that point may not respond properly; someone else may have a technical problem. And we'll get an average of eight in a group. That's from our panel. If it's a client list or a phone list we will over-recruit because we don't have the same relationship with the people on a client or telephone list as we do with people on our panel. We don't know as much about them.

WALKOWSKI Okay, suppose we've recruited people, and they show up for the groups. I am now going to ask a question that I hear from clients: How can you be sure that the respondents who show up are who they say they are?

ROTH I'd say this goes back to screening and rescreening, and the initial invitations sent to people who sign up for our panel or are on the client list. And then when you get into the groups, you can find out. I can tell you that I've never had a person who was obviously the wrong person. I've had people who show up the night of groups who have been screened out because they've shown up for their husband or their brother, but they've told us that.

KLUG [Humorous aside] Well, we use fingerprints and DNA testing.

WEBER In many cases the topic is very specific. You're not going to have a teenager come in to talk about what physicians are supposed to be dealing with. So I think that you can quickly weed out the fraudulent people.

WALKOWSKI Let's say I'm a physician, and I've been recruited. And all of a sudden something comes up, and I can't make it to the scheduled session. I know there's two hundred bucks in my pocket that's at stake. And I let my colleague know my password. Are there any safeguards available to prevent that from happening; so you know it's me, the one that you recruited, who's participating, and not another physician that I have recruited to take my place?

KINDIG I would say it's sort of the same situation that Susan [Roth] gave before, the screening and rescreening. We've had cheaters and repeaters in face-to-face groups, too. And we have very unusual respondents that can show up face-to-face as well. I think that's the process that we rely on, and, as Dan [Weber] says, so much of the research is targeted. I think people would be bored if they weren't qualified to have the discussion. It's actually fairly boring to sit and watch these if you don't have an investment in the topic.

ROTH I guess we're all saying there's no 100 percent answer.

WALKOWSKI That's what I'm hearing, too. Okay. Somebody mentioned something about observers. I'd be interested in your perspectives on what you hear from your observers about what the experience is like.

ESIPOVA I find it very positive in online focus groups. Observers can ask their extra questions right away. In a traditional focus group observers sit behind a one-way mirror, and at the very end of the group, someone shows up with a piece of paper with the observers' extra questions. You may be so far from the topic at that point that it's hard to go back to a previous topic with the participants. Usually we don't get a lot from this indirect observer involvement with the group. With online focus groups, if it's a reasonable question from the observers, you can ask it right away. That's a big positive point for online groups.

ROTH I could say generally clients have been very happy, but it's really a matter of managing their expectations. If what they are expecting is something that very closely resembles a traditional focus group, they might not be happy with an online group. We do ninety-minute online groups, whereas most traditional groups are two hours. Because you (as moderator) are typing and the respondents are reading answers, writing back, reading what's happening, you can only cover so much material. You cover less ground in an online group than in a traditional group. In an online bulletin board you cover more ground. Generally, I would say clients are very happy. It's a matter of setting their expectations appropriately.

WALKOWSKI How do you set their expectations?

ROTH I try to find out, first of all, whether the clients are comparing a project to another that was done traditionally. That's a red flag right there. We need to look at what they can expect. It's really a matter of looking at the discussion guide in terms of what can be covered realistically, and asking them to set priorities.

WALKOWSKI What do you tell your clients beforehand in order to prepare them for their first observation session in an online group?

ESIPOVA They can try the software to become familiar with it. Otherwise it will be trouble for them the first time.

KINDIG For first-time client-users we would offer a training session specifically for them. The clients can come to experience the software, have a demonstration, get an explanation, and have their expectations set. Because I think we're all out to have everybody be happy with the outcome.

KLUG One of the best ways (particularly for people who are new to online technology) is to set up a focus group online that involves just the observers. Invite them to participate as panelists, and then also switch back and forth between the observation room and the focus group room. In a short time they get a feeling for the technique and the application. I think that in itself can set expectations about how to approach your discussion guide, how you want to budget your time, and how you're going to probe and use the moderator effectively.

WEBER The general feedback we've received is that they think it's great.

WALKOWSKI What do they say is great about it?

WEBER I think part of it is the clients being able to collaborate with one another in multinational companies. They're having a fun time chatting in the back room while this thing is taking place. There is a bit of a novelty that's still there, but the feedback is that the information that they're getting is excellent.

KLUG Probably the best thing is they're not sitting in an airport; they're sitting in their living rooms.

ROTH Also, I suggest that clients pass the discussion guide around prior to the group because once they find out how easy it is to access the moderator, people tend to jump in sending messages to the moderator from the observation room. Everybody has a question to ask. Giving everybody on the client team the discussion guide in advance ensures that everything they want covered will be covered. In addition, I usually suggest that, if there are many people in the observation room, one person be designated to give questions to the moderator because it can become a free-for-all with too many observers.

2.5 Myths

WALKOWSKI Okay, let's switch topics. What are the biggest myths of online qualitative research?

KINDIG That it's a replacement technology, rather than a new tool for people to use.

WALKOWSKI How is that a myth? Explain.

KINDIG There are some people out there who think that online research is being positioned as a partial or total replacement for face-to-face research. That's, in fact, a myth. Online research represents an incremental opportunity to conduct research rather than a replacement technology for what currently exists.

KLUG I agree.

WALKOWSKI Well, let me ask you this. Is it likely that the research would not have been done if online qualitative were not available to us? If you're saying it's incremental, then that means that it probably wouldn't have been done. So I'm trying to figure out if that is, in fact, what's going on.

WEBER I think that might be the case. We're not finding people saying, "Should I do this online, or should I do it offline?" The only case is perhaps when they are hesitant about the methodology, when they're not comfortable with it yet. It's not a decision about whether this research would be better online or not. I think it's pretty cut and dried in most cases to the people that are doing it. And they don't have any trouble choosing online once they are comfortable with the technology.

KINDIG I think particularly about research that we've done for Web applications, site identification, usability, and other types of Web evaluations. They're just so much more potent and powerful online than they are in face-to-face groups, because, in fact, you're testing the media in the environment in which it is intended to be used. That's an example of one where I feel like the online medium strongly contributes to the quality of the research as opposed to choosing to do it in an offline environment.

WALKOWSKI Again, choosing to play devil's advocate, though, some usability researchers would say that we need to see what they're doing. Yes, put them online, but put them in front of our machines at a central location. Or let me go see them at their offices or homes, and watch what they're doing. Because if I can't see exactly what they're doing, I might miss out on an opportunity to figure out what's really going on.

KLUG Then, obviously, you should do that. That's really the answer. What are your objectives? What are you trying to accomplish? Structure your research, your methodology, to meet those needs. And if you want to see people, to watch their body language, then you need to get in a room with them. Then you're not going to use this online methodology. I think that gets at this myth of online replacing traditional face-to-face methods. It's so obvious that you can't do that. If you want to see people's eyes roll, then you better get in a room with them.

ROTH There are also instances where it's appropriate to do both. Do the groups in person; see what they're doing. But then, also, do some groups that are online in order to have people at their own computers in their own homes and working in their own environment.

KINDIG That's a really good point. And I can also think of other research that we've done that actually couldn't have been done without online methods. (Well, I suppose it could have been done by telephone interviewing, for example. But then we would have lost out on the dynamic of the group setting, which for the objectives was desirable.) I'm thinking particularly with non-ambulatory and geographically dispersed patients, for example, with whom we've done research. And we probably wouldn't have even proposed to do studies had we not had options that let us bring people collectively together that were scattered very far apart.

WALKOWSKI Any other myths or misconceptions about online qualitative?

ESIPOVA I've heard many times that people are resistant to online focus groups because they think that there is not enough interaction among participants. Again, I want to mention our research with the A. C. Nielsen Center for Marketing Research. What our research showed was that there was no difference in interaction across online, face-to-face, and telephone modalities. There is variability among focus groups within each modality, but not between modalities per se. What this means is that in some focus groups you can see great chemistry among the participants. We had one online focus group in which people just didn't want to leave. They were exchanging e-mail addresses. They were speaking with each other politely. We literally had to tell them that we had to go home. Meaningful interaction can happen in any modality. And, yes, when you're in an online focus group, you have to be very creative to encourage interaction, but you have the same task in face-to-face and in telephone focus groups.

WEBER I think one other thing that is a myth is that people are unable to express their feelings through written or typed words. And from our findings, that simply isn't true. Tell that to William Shakespeare. People can express their feelings online. You know quite well what a person's reaction is and how he or she is feeling as part of the group. And the clients are telling us that that is the case.

WALKOWSKI Getting back to interaction, does it just happen naturally, or does it need to be encouraged? And if it needs to be encouraged, how does that happen?

ESIPOVA Both. There are both components in it. First it's chemistry among participants, and, again, I think that is true in any modality. Secondly, it's one of the skills of the moderator to be able to encourage interaction in the right form and the right place, and not to be too pushy at the same time.

WALKOWSKI **Other comments?**

KINDIG I just thought of another myth. And I think this will be interesting, because I don't know if it's a myth for everybody. There is a positioning that online qualitative is faster, better, cheaper. In our case, it is not cheaper. It's cheaper if you save on travel costs, and the honoraria or incentives may be slightly less expensive. But I will charge you the same amount for design, moderating, analysis, and reporting as I would for a face-to-face group. So, the difference in costs are not as extreme (at least if you're using my organization) as I think people expect they might be.

ESIPOVA I agree. And you actually spent much more time to set it up, to put up the questions in the discussion guide; so you can click and cut and paste during the online focus group session. But at the same time, I would say that at the stage of reporting and analysis it might be easier to analyze online focus groups because the transcript is clean and you have the name of each participant every time he or she types a response. For face-to-face or telephone transcriptions you cannot always understand who was talking. And if it's important to you to know exactly who is talking, it's a real problem.

WALKOWSKI **I'd still like to hear a little bit more about the interaction issue.**

KLUG Another factor in the interaction is the experience of the participants in chat rooms. We oftentimes get people into these things who are not experienced chatters and probably do not have very good keyboard skills as well. So it takes them a while to get used to being able to type in a message.

WALKOWSKI **Do you ever screen for previous chat room experience?**

KLUG I don't recall that we ever have done that because we're more interested in their behavior with regard to the products and services being researched. And our assumption is that it's easy enough to adapt to the technology, that you'll be able to pick it up fairly quickly. But it does take you a little bit, and the skill of the moderator is important in being able to draw people in and get them to participate and get them over that. There are other things that go on, particularly, depending upon the technology that you're using. It takes a little bit of time getting used to the screen refreshing, the way that it scrolls, and things of that sort. If you're not familiar with chat, you're going to need a little bit of time to get up to speed.

ROTH It's primarily up to the moderator to set the tone and to give permission to people to interact and to be a little bit playful. You let them know that it's okay to have fun with this group. That frees people up to agree and disagree and to play off of each other. That has to be done within reason, of course. But it's usually quite effective to just give people permission to speak up.

ESIPOVA Another way of increasing interaction is to use your waiting room time. What I mean by this is that (as in a traditional focus group) people are arriving early in a waiting room. To help them relax you can give them information or ask them a question. Tell them what they have in common, for example. After that you can disappear, and they start talking with each other. So by the time you bring them into the focus group, they already have become acquainted.

WALKOWSKI True or false? A good face-to-face moderator equals a good online moderator.

WEBER We work with many moderators. We can't say for certain that's the case. There are some moderators that are very experienced traditionally that don't want to come near a computer. The general consensus from our standpoint, though, is that the experienced moderators tend to pick up the technology more quickly and understand it and use it well. It's not the case that you can bring in someone who is "green" and has never moderated a group before and expect him or her to be able to take on this technology and be able to handle it. It does involve the skill of being an experienced moderator.

ESIPOVA I can tell you what I think successful face-to-face and online focus group moderators have. It's a sense of humor. Just to keep people alive it does help to have a good sense of humor and to know when you can use it. And that goes for all modalities.

KINDIG I think it's important to emphasize what Dan [Weber] said—and this goes in the myth category, too—there is a myth that anyone can moderate a chat session. That's not what this is. So I would say that having qualitative research skills and moderating skills are the first requirement, and then understanding how to adapt those skills for the specific technology that you're using is a second-level skill set that is needed in order to be successful in conducting these types of groups.

KLUG I would say that chances are that if you're a good moderator face-to-face, after you do this about three or four times, you're going to be a good online focus group moderator. I'd also say that if you're a good chat moderator, that doesn't necessarily make you a good research moderator. The effective moderator is the one who understands what your objectives are and knows how to adapt "on the fly" as the group is unfolding. Deviate a bit from the discussion guide if that's what it's going to take to draw people out. That's where the skill comes in.

ROTH I think we're all in agreement on that. I'd also say that most of the tutorials that I've seen for doing online moderating have been about understanding the online environment, understanding the online consumer and the use of the software. They're not about teaching moderation skills. We are expecting online moderators to come with basic moderator skills.

WALKOWSKI Any other misconceptions or myths that you can think of?

KINDIG I'll offer one more idea. I don't think that it's always faster. I think that if you are looking to talk with general consumers and you have very few qualifying criteria for doing the research, it can be very quick and easy to find people who meet those conditions and bring them together. But, on the other hand, if you're trying to bring together a panel of high-level experts to talk, that can take as long or longer to recruit as traditional research. So the positioning that this is always faster and cheaper does a disservice to the methodology. It's like all research. It can be many different things.

WALKOWSKI Some of the misconceptions that you mentioned fall into the category of barriers or resistance to using the online methodology. What other sources of resistance, or what other barriers, have you encountered in trying to sell or propose online qualitative?

ESIPOVA Lack of facial expression—that's a big concern for clients. And, as we mentioned before, if that's what you want, you might want to go for face-to-face. But by doing online focus groups you can enhance some expressions by telling people up front, please, if you want to smile, draw a smiley face, or if you are angry, put your answer in capital letters when you type your response. What you don't have with facial expressions, you might have in the text because people use different words. Online words are usually stronger than face-to-face words. So you have to look at the analysis a bit differently to get the same outcome.

WALKOWSKI Other responses to this? Agree or disagree?

KLUG I don't disagree, but I thought of another area that is a bit of a barrier, depending upon the client. And that is this idea of confidentiality on the Web. Let's say that you want to get a group of medical professionals and you want to talk about the formulas for Viagra, and you're going to put this up on the white board section of your session. Regardless of what you do, you're on the Web. The whole principle behind the Web is openness. So there is a barrier there. A security officer for a pharmaceutical company might just raise the red flag and say, "You're not going to do this, you're not going to put this kind of information on the Web. And I don't care if you're behind a secure packet layer and three other levels of password protection, it's not going to be transmitted across an open line, whether it's encrypted or not."

WALKOWSKI And what do you say in that case? What's your response?

KLUG Don't do it on the Web. You're absolutely right. Just get them in a room and see if you can do a memory erase if you're really concerned about it.

WALKOWSKI Do you personally feel that those concerns are justified?

KLUG I would say that if the client has those concerns, yes, absolutely. I might try to demonstrate that this is a secure environment and that there is little risk. But it could be a show-stopper. And you say, "Okay, we're not going to do it." We're certainly not going to push it to the point where that client's uncomfortable with it.

WEBER I think one of the biggest barriers right now is that many of the research companies are deciding whether or not they should expose their clients to this technology. They still have fears about whether the technology will work. "Is my client going to get what he wants out of this? And will that affect my entire portfolio with this client?" I think as more and more groups are being done on a regular basis, as the technology is getting better and as the reporting and analysis is getting better, we're going to see more acceptance of online products. As opposed to, "Here's something that we can try if we're interested." At this point what we're seeing is client-driven. "We have this product, it's tucked away, and if the client asks for it, we'll bring it out." Obviously, I'm interested in changing that type of attitude. But that's where I see it right now.

ROTH And I think, also, as we have clients run more parallel studies where they can see how research results compare online versus offline, comfort levels will continue to grow, and usage will too.

WALKOWSKI I'd like to go back to the confidentiality issue. If a client I'm dealing with has any trepidation about security, I say, "Hey, no problem, let's figure out some other way." Do you feel that their fears about the risks associated with confidentiality are justified, or do you just acquiesce to their position and feel that they just don't get it?

KINDIG I feel that in many cases their fears are justified when dealing in a highly competitive environment. The software tools that we use are disabled from respondents being able to print anything out. But there's no way to disable a keyboard from doing a screen capture. There's physically no way to disable that. So if you have a highly confidential concept that you are proposing in a highly competitive industry, I wouldn't recommend online research because I don't want to put my client at risk for having that information exposed.

WALKOWSKI Other thoughts?

ROTH I would say that if clients are concerned about it, given that they know more about their industry and its competitive nature and what's happening in their industry than we do, then it's our ethical obligation to steer them in another direction (away from online). We had a client in the automotive industry that was considering showing prototypes of cars online and asked about security. We told them exactly what we could promise, and what we could not promise.

WALKOWSKI And what was that?

ROTH Well, we can try to screen for the right people, and we've got encryption software and secure software. There are things we can do. But we can't stop someone from printing a screen or taking a Polaroid of a screen. There are things that are impossible for us to control. And in this case millions of dollars were at stake. So, I don't think we had a choice there.

KLUG The security on the Internet is an interesting topic. And the best way to think about it in my mind is that if you're willing to take this information and send it to somebody in the mail, then you're okay doing it on the Internet. If you wouldn't do that, then don't do Internet research, because you're essentially taking this information and you're putting it outside of your control. And when you put it on the Web, no matter what kind of encryption application you have, like Susan [Roth] mentioned, I'll take my little digital camera and take a snapshot of the screen, and I've got your image. So if you're not concerned about that level of security, then you can do it. But if you're not going to mail it out, don't consider doing it on the Web.

2.6 Areas for Improvement

WALKOWSKI As researchers, what are some of the problems that you have with online qualitative?

KLUG Problems?

WALKOWSKI Yes. What are some of the things that happen in the course of doing an online project that if they went away, it would make your life so much easier?

KLUG I would say that making sure that you've got the right people in your group, people that qualify. That's probably where if a group is going to fail, it's because you either weren't clear about the kind of behavior you were trying to get or you didn't frame your screening questions properly. And you get them into the group and you find out that these really aren't the people that I would like to talk to, and you go back and do it again and try to find the right people. But that's probably one of the more frequent types of problems that we would run into. You've just got to really think through how to identify the people you're looking for and make sure you're screening properly.

WALKOWSKI Is that a problem that you see more in online qualitative than traditional qualitative?

KLUG I really can't speak for that. I think probably it would be a problem in any form of recruitment like that. But I would say that that's one of the problems that we really need to look for and guard for.

ESIPOVA Technical issues.

WALKOWSKI Such as?

ESIPOVA If someone gets disconnected. In face-to-face, even if the lights turn off, you can keep talking. As with telephone groups, people don't see each other. But if you lose a person online, first of all, it's a big struggle for the person to come back, and secondly, you're losing time. And if you promise people that you are doing the focus group for one-and-a-half hours, you have to keep your promise.

ROTH Yes.

WALKOWSKI To what extent does that happen?

ESIPOVA It happened to us a few times last year. It doesn't happen very often, but it does happen; so you have to be prepared for this.

WEBER As more people consolidate browsers and as we put more time and effort into designing the software, we've overcome quite a number of those technical barriers. Beyond that, though, you have to develop support structures around the software itself to deal with the technical issues. You have to provide an 800 line for people to call. And maybe the problem is just as simple as a person typing his password improperly. And obviously, technical problems can drastically affect the client's perception of this type of methodology. So developing systems that support the group is as important as the technology and method that you're using.

WALKOWSKI Other issues that you have as providers? [No response from panelists.] **So doing online qualitative is a piece of cake.**

KINDIG Well, I don't know if this is what you're looking for or not. Maybe this is a methodological constraint rather than an online constraint. I think about the fact that I do a lot of work in branding and brand personality and things like that. It involves a lot of very creative projective techniques that involve a lot of hands-on work, a lot of looking at projective pictures, collaging. And I can't do that, obviously, online. There are projective techniques that I can use online and I have, but just by the very nature of it, online research is more constrained, more limited. So I guess, for me, in a way maybe that's a methodological constraint, but the inability to do those types of really creative interventions is problematic.

WALKOWSKI Can you dream on that and tell us what, ideally, you would like to be able to do online that you can't do today?

KINDIG Well, that goes to my crystal ball. I think with home access to broadband on the rise, with individuals investing in technology (as technology prices decrease), we're going to be moving to combinations of voice and text, as well as video, voice, and text, for online research. Text-only is probably an interim technology that's on its way to evolving. And that would go to addressing some of those issues.

WALKOWSKI How would those evolutions help you?

KINDIG For me, I could engage respondents in activities that required me to see what they were doing at their end. So, for example, I could ask people to do homework assignments or I could ask them to do things in the course of the group. They could be assembling pictures and stories and things that I'm asking them to show and share with the group that are an integral part of the discussion. So that would be very helpful to me.

WALKOWSKI Let's move on to the crystal ball, then. Where do you see things headed with online qualitative? Or where would you like them to head?

ESIPOVA I would like to see more acceptance among researchers of online focus groups. But it's the same with resistance to all online research. There are many people who are still very skeptical about it.

WALKOWSKI Do you think it will change, or will it stay the way it is today?

ESIPOVA It's the same as with online survey research. Some people will change their opinions, and some will not.

WALKOWSKI Other forecasts?

WEBER I think that we'll see migration. We can compare it to the telephone and initial reaction to when the telephone came in to being used for interview research. There was a push back. Then it started being integrated. And eventually people see the new technology as a viable means of conducting research. We're just starting to see that take place now. If your competition is doing good research, there's only so long they can sit there and say, "Well, you know, the methodology is flawed."

ROTH As the demographics of people on the Internet more closely match the population, we will see more acceptance. But also, as Lisa [Kindig] just mentioned, as broadband increases that will affect new avenues for us in terms of videoconferencing, wireless applications, hardware in kitchens, various things. I think it's going to be a very exciting time in the years to come. There will be a lot of new opportunities available to us.

WALKOWSKI In one of the panels at the 2000 EXPLOR Forum yesterday, some numbers were floated about the percentage of research that will be captured by online. And my understanding is that the percentages that were floated related to the quantitative side of the business. First of all, does anybody have any idea what percentage of all qualitative work is done online? I'm not aware of any numbers, I'm wondering if you are.

KLUG I don't know of any.

WALKOWSKI [No response from other panelists.] **I take that as a "no." Okay.**

KINDIG Well, actually, as part of the crystal ball that I see, this is part of it. I see metrics being evaluated and studies being done to understand the penetration of online qualitative research. I also see standards of practice being established with the work, for example, from such organizations as the Qualitative Research Consultants Association, in combination with CASRO, ESOMAR, and IMRO. As people are aware, there are already CASRO standards for online research, but they pertain primarily to quantitative research. So we are missing, currently, standards that apply specifically to qualitative. As part of the development of those standards, I would imagine that some of this data about incidence and penetration would be quantified for qualitative.

WALKOWSKI If you had to take a stab at it, what percentage of all qualitative research done in this country would you say is done online? Does anybody feel comfortable giving a number?

WEBER Less than half of a percent.

WALKOWSKI Less than half of 1 percent. Anybody think it's any higher than that? Okay. I've heard a "yes" at my left over here. Let's say five years from now. Take a stab at it. Where do you think it might be? Let's assume that it is a half a percent now.

KLUG I think five years from now we'll be talking about an entirely different set of tools for collaborative thinking and collaborative capturing of ideation and things of that sort. Right now, we're using chat and bulletin boards, technologies that have been around for quite some time as the Internet has evolved. I think that we just have to get our imaginations cranked up to figure out how we're really going to expand the horizons of ways that we communicate with people in a group setting, collaboratively to get at ideas that researchers and product managers are trying to understand about their products and services. And I don't think that we can sit here and say that there's a percentage of what we do today that is really appropriate for five years from now, because I think the base is going to be a lot different.

WEBER I think if you look at qualitative as a whole, including these methodologies, I'm willing to guess that 20 to 25 percent in the next five years will be done online.

WALKOWSKI What do you base that on?

WEBER Partly history in our own research, working with market research companies over the past three years and the growth rate that we're experiencing now. So that's what I base those projections on. And I guess the capabilities that now come into play with the broadband and other areas as well.

ROTH That sounds pretty reasonable to me, but I also agree with Bernie [Klug] that it's going to be a whole new ball game five years from now.

WALKOWSKI Can you elaborate on that?

ROTH All I can say is that we can't predict right now what the Internet will look like and what else there will be besides the Internet. So I don't think we'll just be working with the Internet.

2.7 Audience Questions and Answers

WALKOWSKI As promised, we've got about ten minutes left before the break, and I would be happy to hand the microphone to anybody who has questions.

ATTENDEE A I have two questions I think could take the whole session. The first one is: I'm wondering if any of you validate any of your online research, comparing online focus group findings with quantitative research? And the second question: (I found myself thinking it is fashionable today to do online research, whatever it is.) A lot of the online focus group benefits seem to be benefits you could get with telephone conference calls. Could we get a lot of similar information on the telephone?

ESIPOVA In the study we conducted, we did have telephone focus groups. We had the same results, the same management learnings, across modalities. There were differences in several areas across modalities. Lengths of speech segments, for example. I don't want to go into the details, but I can tell you that when we did a survey with participants after conducting the focus groups, the main complaint was about telephone focus groups. What participants didn't like was that they didn't know when they could speak. So they immediately tried to establish an order of speaking. You don't have that with face-to-face groups because with face-to-face it's easier for people to take turns. They don't have the feeling that they are interrupting someone. They are very uncomfortable with it on telephone focus groups. Telephone focus groups with the same content as online or face-to-face groups are usually shorter. What takes one hour and thirty minutes for face-to-face groups will take one hour and ten minutes for telephone groups. The outcome (the management learning) is the same across the three modalities. The problem is that participants don't like the telephone modality very much.

WEBER In the telephone group, you still have to have a means of presenting your stimuli if you are planning to show anything. You still have to have some other application in place that everyone is using.

KINDIG Also, the telephone groups have the same limitation as chat-style groups and face-to-face groups that the bulletin board overcomes, which is requiring people to come together at one time. So it's very nice to have an alternative online methodology that doesn't require that. In addition, an advantage of the online chat versus telephone is that you can embed exercises into your online focus groups. You're not able to do that sort of thing with telephone groups. (And, by the way, I like telephone groups, and I do them.)

WALKOWSKI Can you give an example of that? What can you do online that you can't do over the phone? An exercise. Just one example, please.

KINDIG You can take votes, for example, and everybody has to register his or her response before hearing what others say. So that's similar to a face-to-face group where everybody writes down his or her response. So you're getting individual effects as well as the group dynamic. Whereas in a telephone group, you can't physically do that.

ESIPOVA You can show the video online. You cannot do that over the phone.

ATTENDEE B My company is planning multiple, simultaneous, worldwide discussions. You didn't talk too much about analysis. I'm wondering what the leading edge is for activity analysis and report writing. In the online situation you have an instant transcript, which I take to be a big advantage.

So what are the value-added tools that are on the market (or that you are offering) to take advantage of this readily accessible text? And how are you measuring activity in new ways?

ROTH What do you mean by measuring activity?

ATTENDEE B Well, in the online situation you have measures of how long a person is there and what he or she says. You quantify it. To some extent you quantify the qualitative. So what's available that you're offering in that area? And also, the text analysis is a different topic, but I put that in the area of reporting.

WEBER Text analysis (just in terms of the transcript and what we receive) is a lot more detailed from what is being transcribed from traditional groups. We can indicate where a comment is coming from (whether it is in the client room or the focus group room). Everything is time-stamped. So we know how long it took for people to produce answers. The instantaneous transcript allows you to do analysis right away. The transcript itself is much easier to use and more versatile.

KINDIG Maybe I take a different approach than others, but I can get transcripts within twenty-four hours in face-to-face groups; so for me having them available at 10:00 P.M. at night after the group versus 5:00 P.M. the next day is not that much different for me. And my analytical techniques are frankly not very different because for me it's all text. That's what I'm receiving. Right now, I can tell you that among all the qualitative researchers that I've talked to (and I'd be interested if anyone else has a different experience), no one has had what he or she would consider to be successful experience with any text analysis software that does keyword searches and things like that. This is because people are often speaking contextually, and they're not using keywords when they're talking. So often it's simply a matter of doing a full review of the transcript, just as you would from audio-transcribed work. So for me the text analysis process is not particularly different between online and face-to-face groups. I have different tools that are multimedia tools that I use with audio-recorded groups.

ATTENDEE C My interest is apparel and the fashion trendsetter. Are we at a place where we can do focus groups where individuals who might be trendsetters can show everybody over the Internet what they're wearing and be able to have a group discussion about that?

KLUG That capability is not generally available, but it will certainly become available when you start to see broadband applications with people who have video cameras in their equipment and have the ability to do streaming video in a peer-to-peer discussion like that. I think that's one of those future things that's somewhere down the line. But right now, I think broadband penetration is less than 5 percent. So if you're looking for general population kinds of audiences, you're probably going to have a tough time finding them. But trendsetter apparel people sound like they might be on the upper echelon of the income structure. So that might work in your favor.

ROTH That's actually not just an issue, though, of finding people with broadband capacity, but it's an issue of having many people online viewing and receiving images at the same time.

KINDIG But now here's a thought, and this is how online gets exciting. It's actually a whole issue of assembling that panel, which is typically how it's done with trend spotters. So you're convening a panel of people with whom you're going to speak on a regular basis about pre-identifying trends. You could provide incentives by giving them the technology that allows them to participate in online research. So online impacts how we provide incentives to people. I can see, for example, as broadband gains greater access, providing people with fifty-dollar Web cameras, so that they could then participate in a conferenced focus group. We would do this rather than cutting them a check or sending them a T-shirt, or whatever, if, in fact, that segment's feedback is valuable to the research.

WALKOWSKI Time for one more question.

ATTENDEE D What about technology on the consumer side, things like modem speed, the kind of computer monitors participants have, and the quality of color, et cetera? Technology has a great impact when you're doing things like concept testing. You're trying to make sure that people get equal time and everyone has similar speeds in getting through to the group. How do you deal with the potential inequities on the consumer end?

KLUG One obvious way to do that is that you limit your audience to people who have adequate technology and adequate modem speeds; so that they're not going to be suffering from low-powered Internet access or low-powered computers. If you're using a simple JPEG that is twenty kilobytes in size to get the concept idea across, you can usually do that without having to worry too much about modem speed. But if you are going to embed 3D objects and streaming video or do some of those kinds of things while conducting online groups, then you better limit your audience and make sure that they're qualified participants before you bring them into the group. So that's one way to do it. In earlier days that started to narrow your field and cut some people out that you might have been interested in talking to. But as the cost of technology has gone down, technology becomes less of a problem. I think the last number I saw was that over 60 percent of the people that we interviewed had modem speeds of fifty-six kilobits per second and above. Whereas a year-and-a-half ago, two years ago, I think that number was 20 percent. Of course, fifty-six kilobits per second is not going to be very fast pretty soon. But there are enough people out there now that have high-speed modems; so you can do most of the kinds of things that we've talked about very comfortably.

2.8 Epilogue

Nearly three years have passed since the above panel discussion was conducted. While many of the points made by these panelists remain true today, there have been changes in the environment of qualitative research online. This section offers some perspective on what has changed and what has not changed.

It is difficult to say how much qualitative research is conducted online. Measures of market size are lacking. But we believe that expenditures for qualitative research online remain a small part of total qualitative research expenditures. Drawing upon Studies of Information Research and Consulting Services, Miller and James (2003) note that focus groups and in-depth interviews are much less likely to be conducted online than with traditional methods. Concept and copy testing, which often include qualitative components, are more frequently conducted online. Table 2.1 shows reported usage of research types by research providers and users in 2002. The corresponding trellis plot in Figure 2.1 shows research types ordered by the frequency of use of traditional methods among providers.

Many barriers remain to the application of qualitative research online. There is a segment of the research community which does not believe that useful information can be gained from online focus groups. They feel they would be giving up too much by not seeing body language and hearing voice inflection. They imply that without those visual and auditory cues, the qualitative researcher risks drawing incorrect conclusions from the data. In essence, they challenge the external validity of the online research approach.

There is a perceived risk of having proprietary information, such as new product ideas, leaked to people outside the firm. While protections are in place to prevent outsiders from hacking or eavesdropping into an online session, no virtual facility vendor can prevent respondents from capturing images by printing screens or taking photographs of the computer screens.

Another security issue remains. At brick-and-mortar focus group facilities, rescreening is fairly standard practice. Respondent identities and responses to key qualifying questions are checked to be sure that recruited individuals belong in the focus group. Some virtual facility vendors offer methods to reduce the opportunity for imposters to participate in online sessions. While the risk is reduced by verification methods, no virtual facility vendor or online qualitative researcher is able to guarantee with 100 percent certainty that respondents in an online session are exactly who researchers think they are.

What has changed since the panel met? Access to the Internet, including high-speed access, has increased. The online population more closely matches the general population on key demographic characteristics. Today it is more difficult to make the argument that online qualitative research is invalid because the online population is not representative of the general population.

The economic downturn and increased hassles associated with air travel after September 11, 2001, have forced many organizations to consider online qualitative more seriously. Online research reduces travel requirements and costs. Research

Table 2.1: Applications of Traditional and Online Research in 2002

	Percentage of Organizations Using Research Application and Modality			
	Providers (N = 187)		*Users (N = 27)*	
Research Application	*Traditional*	*Online*	*Traditional*	*Online*
Advertising research	71.7	34.2	63.0	14.8
Brand loyalty/equity research	74.9	36.4	81.5	29.6
Choice studies	48.1	30.5	18.5	11.1
Competitive intelligence studies	29.9	16.6	51.9	14.8
Concept testing	74.3	40.6	77.8	33.3
Conjoint studies	47.1	31.6	29.6	7.4
Copy testing	49.7	23.0	40.7	3.7
Customer satisfaction studies	76.5	43.3	74.1	33.3
Database research	33.2	15.5	37.0	18.5
Distribution channel research	24.6	9.6	40.7	11.1
Employee satisfaction studies	50.3	33.2	37.0	29.6
Focus groups	80.7	17.6	96.3	14.8
In-depth interviews	78.6	12.3	74.1	7.4
Market segmentation studies	73.3	28.9	81.5	14.8
Market share estimation	47.6	19.3	55.6	11.1
Market testing	49.2	12.8	48.1	7.4
New product development research	75.9	36.9	74.1	18.5
Opinion polls	46.5	20.3	22.2	18.5
Pricing studies	60.4	26.7	40.7	7.4
Product positioning studies	69.5	30.5	51.9	14.8
Product usage studies	67.9	31.0	55.6	25.9
Quality testing	23.5	4.3	18.5	7.4
Sales forecasting	18.2	5.9	25.9	3.7
Surveys (attitude and behavior)	80.2	42.8	77.8	44.4
Tracking studies	69.5	25.7	55.6	18.5
Volume forecasting	19.3	5.3	18.5	3.7

Source: Studies of Information, Research, and Consulting Services reported by Miller and James (2003).

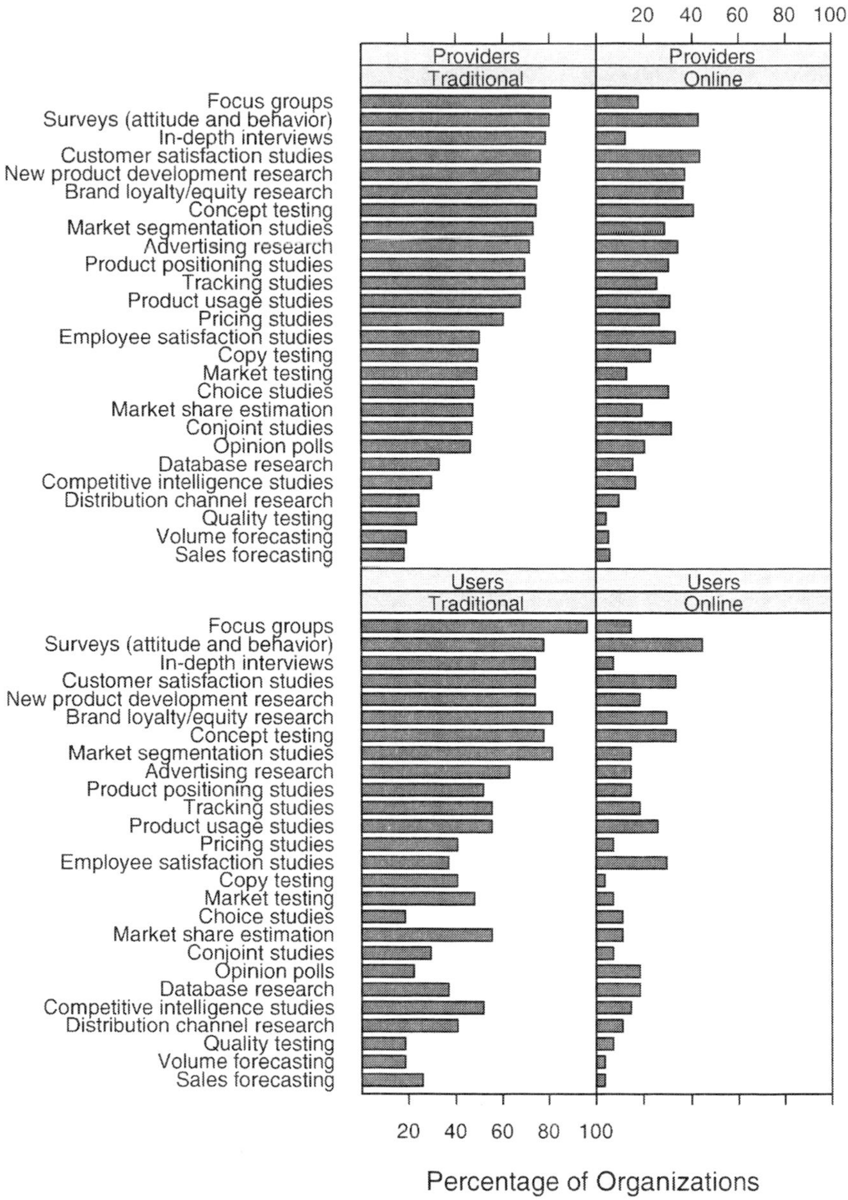

Source: Studies of Information, Research, and Consulting Services reported by Miller and James (2003).

Figure 2.1: Applications of Traditional and Online Research in 2002

buyers mention the joy of being able to observe online focus groups from the comfort of their own homes.

Panel members pointed out that online research seems particularly appropriate for busy professionals, physicians, individuals located in rural areas or foreign countries, those in low incidence groups, and physically handicapped individuals. Since the panel met, there appears to be an increased interest in using online qualitative research methods to bring kids and teens into the research process. This makes sense, given that it has been well documented that children now grow up with the Internet, are highly adept at Internet-based communications, and are quite comfortable using the Internet to communicate with others.

There are signs of growth in online research. While a few virtual facility providers have gone out of business, new facilities have emerged. Competition among online research providers appears to be at work and healthy. Many articles about online qualitative research have appeared in the research press. Training programs have emerged to help skilled moderators adapt to the online arena. These observations suggest that, despite the barriers mentioned by panelists and reiterated above, qualitative research online is considered to be a viable research tool. Qualitative research online is here to stay. Three years after the panel discussion, each of the panelists continues to use online methods.

Chapter 3

Doing Qualitative Research Online

What is it like to conduct qualitative research online? How do researchers feel about the process? What advice do experienced online researchers have for the newcomers? This chapter presents a bulletin board discussion of these and other questions about qualitative research online. Jeff Walkowski served as moderator for the bulletin board discussion. Participants represented qualitative research practitioners with extensive online moderating experience. Appendix C includes their biographies.

We present an edited version of the discussion that took place in May 2001, taking out extraneous banter among participants, rearranging comments to enhance readability, and revising for consistency with American English. All pertinent content remains. Our use of bulletin board software illustrates the utility of this type of qualitative research online. We thank QualTalk.com for providing the virtual focus group facility and technical support for this discussion.

3.1 Prologue

Members of this panel agree that being an online moderator is no easy task. Traditional moderator skills are useful. Reviews of these skills may be found in Krueger (1998), Edmunds (1999), and Langer (2001). In addition to basic moderating skills (guiding the discussion, probing as necessary, not asking leading questions, exhibiting unconditional positive regard), the panelists identify special skills required of online moderators. They provide recommendations for conducting qualitative research online:

- More than in traditional settings, online moderators must be adept at multitasking and quick on their feet.
- The moderator's guide for an online group may be quite different from a moderator's guide for an in-person or telephone group.
- Online moderators must be comfortable dealing with technological challenges.

- Online moderators must be able to read quickly and must have at least minimal keyboarding skills (unless they have an assistant do the typing).
- Without the benefit of seeing respondents and hearing them speak, online moderators must learn to be sensitive to other cues that reveal what respondents are really communicating.
- Include at least one phone conversation with the respondent during the recruitment process to strengthen the likelihood that the recruit will actually show up for the online session. Also, recruiters need to be straightforward and honest with respondents about what is expected of them in the online session.
- Online moderators should adapt their sense of humor, presentation style, word choice, and conversational style to the online environment.
- Online moderators should call each participant by name, keep the participant involved in the conversation, and let the participant know that contributions to the discussion are welcome.
- Online moderators can foster interaction by being playful and by asking for comments about the statements of individual participants.

The panelists contend that public chat room moderators are not necessarily adept at being effective online focus group moderators. Skills of online focus group moderators are akin to skills of online educators involved with computer mediated communication (Salmon 2000). There is a "netiquette" for e-mails and conferences. There are techniques for encouraging participation. There are requirements for keeping discussion focused upon the research topic.

Building on the findings from panelists in the previous chapter, this expert panel identifies barriers to the acceptance of online qualitative research methods. Poor show rates in initial experiences with online qualitative research have discouraged some researchers from using online qualitative research. Some think of bulletin boards as an older and less appealing methodology than real-time chats, affecting the frequency of adoption of these methods. There is debate, even among the expert online researchers on this panel, as to whether to use the term "online focus groups" for what are really text-based online discussions or moderated chats. Some argue that online focus groups are qualitatively different from traditional focus groups.

Panelists predict that the increased penetration of high-speed Internet access (broadband cable and DSL) will permit multimedia options for interventions in online groups and will provide more flexibility to researchers in terms of what types of stimuli can be shown to respondents. Furthermore, some panelists believe that faster access speeds will permit participants (via video and audio hookups) to see and hear each other while online. Note that some panelists argue that being able to see and hear respondents may actually diminish benefits of conducting qualitative research online, such as anonymity and the increased honesty that anonymity can provide.

3.2 Introductions

WALKOWSKI **As with any group discussion, introductions are in order. Tell us about your first online qualitative project.**

LOVEJOY My first experiments with online qualitative were about four years ago when I tried an online focus group using IRC. This was done purely as an experiment to see how it worked. I then experimented with Web-based chat rooms, ICQ, listservs, and Web boards. For reasons which will doubtless emerge in the discussion and which can also be found in my ESOMAR paper (Lovejoy 2000), I make very limited use of what I call virtual focus groups (live chat room groups) but much more use of e-mail groups and Web boards like this one.

BÉLISLE I've come relatively late to online research. I started last year, fell in love with it, and have probably logged some two hundred hours online, both in chat sessions (two dozen or so) and bulletin boards (a half dozen or so). My "first time" was scary and exhilarating. I acted as moderator-for-hire for a large Internet-based research company that handled all aspects of the research except for the moderating and reporting. I was struck by the combination of efficiency and chaos, intensity and remoteness, and resolved to move my consultancy in the direction of more online work.

SWEET About 1996 or so I learned about chat groups online from a software provider that wanted to exhibit at the QRCA conference I was co-chairing. I became interested, but didn't pursue it much until the next year when I got some colleagues online for a demo and immediately fell in love with it. I realized I found myself easily "in relationship" with others and it did not matter that I could not see them. Previously, I had questioned the ability to form connected relationships online. This convinced me that it was possible, and probably even more so for those younger folks who grew up being online. From there I decided the best thing to do was create a full-fledged project from beginning to end for my company so I could learn more. Those groups were the most revealing I have ever conducted because I was able to ask them about their environment, participation, recruitment experience, and other questions not appropriate in typical projects. Later I began working with another online research supplier and learned how to conduct bulletin boards for them as well as my own clients. To date, I have conducted over 150 groups with about a third bulletin boards and two-thirds real-time.

VAN NUYS I certainly am not one of the originators of online qualitative, but I did see the possibility early on. I was trying to interest an advertising agency in the concept before I was aware that any tools had been developed. About three years ago, as a result of finally joining QRCA, I discovered that online tools were already available. I've been doing mostly real-time chat, somewhere between thirty to fifty sessions at this point. I've only done about a half-dozen threaded discussions, so far. I believe my first real-time chat groups were for a well-known online dating service. They were interested in hearing from members of their Associate Program about a number of new issues. Since the Associates were mostly Web masters, the online chat experience came very naturally to them and the group fairly ran itself. I, too, was a bit nervous with the logistics of it all, but it ran smoothly enough, and the client was quite pleased.

ZINCHIAK When I started on my own I was doing mostly traditional focus group moderation and in-depth interviews. I was contacted by a university professor to moderate some groups. This professor was very into new media and was playing around in chat rooms, trying to develop theories of how they could be applied to market research. She saw my strong interest and basically served as my mentor for the first couple of years. I was hooked on the methodology, and online projects just seemed to flow in my direction. I can't tell you how many groups I have conducted online, but I can tell you I've executed about thirty real-time groups in the last twelve months and one bulletin board focus group. I cannot remember my first project. What I do remember is the awful time respondents had with it—technical problems like 14.4 modems, unreliable service providers, and AOL blocking. Oh, how far we have come.

HERBERT I am not a techie but see myself as primarily a social science type of qualitative researcher. I conducted my first online groups—which we call CyberQual—using IRC technology in 1994. My first commercial project was for a U.K. newspaper in early 1995 when they were developing their electronic newspaper. We recruited respondents from around the world as well as from the United Kingdom via the electronic newspaper and conducted face-to-face and online groups in the United Kingdom as well as online groups in the United States, Australia, and some in-depth interviews in Europe. This was extraordinarily exciting stuff at the time. I have conducted fifty or sixty online groups since then. The last major project online was using the same respondents to participate in an online group and a face-to-face group with two separate discussion guides across four life-stage groups. This proved to be very interesting comparing their responses and attitudes toward face-to-face groups and online groups. This is my first message board and while Ben [Lovejoy] tells me e-mail groups are really exciting, I've never done one. But I can't help feeling it would be like doing a real life group using letters rather than getting together in real time, but I'm open to persuasion.

WINTER With regard to online work, early on I was one of the naysayers: "You can't see the body language; they don't know you're a dog when you're on the Internet." But, when I realized that online focus groups should not be looked at as a replacement for traditional groups, I started seriously investigating the medium. We put up our own virtual room in 1998 and while our online quantitative side got rolling more quickly, the qualitative side has been experiencing nice steady growth. We've spent a lot of time answering questions and educating prospective clients, but it's been worth the price of entry. I'm particularly interested in this bulletin board approach because I see it as a brand new methodology. We've done somewhere around seventy-five real-time chat groups—our only qualitative online experience. Ah, yes—the first online group—I was scared to death that everything that could go wrong technically (bear in mind, it's our own virtual room) would go wrong. It actually was quite smooth, and I had the foresight to have someone else do the typing. I think that really helped in beginning to learn the rhythm of the online group.

SABENA More than two years ago, a marketing researcher and friend of mine told me about a new virtual facility. One of the people from that company came to my house, demonstrated the software, and I was hooked. As soon as the facility was ready, I signed up for training and loved it immediately. I've done about sixteen chat room sessions (six or seven projects), and one week-long bulletin board. I'm very enthusiastic about online research, but have only been partially successful in selling it to clients. The first project was given to me by the virtual facility, so online was the obvious method. It was about Web site enhancement of an existing Web site. The recruiting was done from the site's hits and was quite good. Based on the chat room sessions, the company made immediate and successful changes to the Web site for improved navigation and more engaging content.

3.3 Online Venue Preferences

WALKOWSKI Think of three currently available methods/venues for conducting online qualitative research: real-time chats, message boards, and listserv discussions. Which of the three do you prefer to moderate? Which of the three do you think clients prefer? And which of the three do you think respondents prefer?

LOVEJOY I think many of us looked to real-time chats with great optimism when we first started playing with them. The idea of not having to flog up and down the M1, and being able to avoid getting up at 4:00 A.M. to catch the first flight out to whatever country is next on the list, was hugely appealing. I really, really wanted them to work. It was thus a real disappointment to see what limited insight they actually offer compared to traditional focus groups. I do think they have their place, but they are not the great alternative we hoped they might be. The question gets slightly easier to answer in terms of clients and respondents. I think clients, too, got very excited by chat rooms, and some still are, but I think the novelty value is wearing off. I think Web boards are more tangible than e-mail groups, so I'd say most clients relate best to those. Mass-market consumers tend to like chat rooms. It's a limited time commitment, and again the novelty value is there. Techies tend to prefer e-mail, viewing the Web as less efficient. Business respondents tend to prefer Web boards, as they offer the convenience of anytime-access but often only require them to type a paragraph or two per day for maybe a week.

BÉLISLE I have no preference between chats or boards, though I feel that moderating chats is more stressful and more challenging: this is real time (with the possibility of a real-time disaster), the moderator has to pay really close attention to the chat stream, and there is a need to be thinking on your feet (or with your fingers, I suppose) that approximates the exhilaration of a face-to-face focus group. By contrast, I like the depth of response of message groups, and the way in which participants become literate and literary in describing experiences or proposing/defending points of view. To me, the bulletin board is a much more cerebral tool. Participants are dealing with ideas and how to express them, rather than reacting to a text stream. Clients, however, are not taken by the boards: message boards are static, nothing's happening, and there is no interaction. In fact, I've been surprised and disappointed to see how few (and how infrequently) clients have logged into their observation rooms, preferring to wait for the final report. It would be interesting to ask participants who had participated in both how they felt about chats versus boards. I suspect that their reactions would mirror those of observers. The exception might be specialists or those with a keen interest in whatever topic is being discussed.

VAN NUYS I've read both Ben [Lovejoy] and Pierre [Bélisle]'s responses and have similar reactions. The bulk of my experience, so far, is with real-time chat. In my heart of hearts, I have to say I still prefer to do face-to-face traditional groups. I like the travel, still, and I like the stimulation of interacting with real people and of being "on." At the same time, I like the convenience of chat groups and not having to travel quite so much. I find the chat groups make particular sense for technical topics with technical people. The thing that frustrates me about them is that the responses tend to be very short—one-liners mostly. I find that I have to do lots of reading between the lines—guessing, really. Also, the fact that it is not always clear which question or comment the reply is relating to can be quite frustrating. Threaded discussions, such as this one, do have the benefit of eliciting much longer responses. Case in point, here! :-) So far, however, I've found them to be a harder sell. All of my online groups have been the result of a potential client asking for the chat modality. Although I've been involved in listservs as an academic, I've never tried to use one for qualitative research. I know that I'm very wary of joining listservs because I've learned that one can very quickly become overwhelmed by all the e-mail. Does that become an issue in the market research context?

BÉLISLE Your comment about allocating replies to the right question in chat groups is something that I've also found. It must be amenable to a technical solution. I, too, have found the bulletin boards to be a hard sell. I can't believe, for instance, that companies aren't falling over themselves to empanel some of their key customer groups in quasi-perpetual bulletin boards. Maybe bulletin board groups need a bit more sizzle!

SWEET I agree. I, too, am very surprised that business-to-business companies aren't falling over each other to do bulletin boards. That's where I think the biggest opportunity is in the future. Also, with consumer panels I can think of a number of great uses. My thought has been that real awareness of bulletin board use is very low and since it is "different" than traditional methods, clients are reluctant to take the risk of a new methodology and pay for it. More eye-opening articles will help.

BÉLISLE Yes, it's a funny situation. Everyone and his or her sibling is putting together loyalty programs, and bulletin boards are, to me, one of the most engaging tools around, particularly as you say, for business-to-business clients who are sometimes involved in long-term product design and development. One client I know had developed, internally, a very clever "design round table" for a particular product. The round table involved e-mail, a secure Web site for quantitative product evaluations, a bulletin board for interactions and assignments, and then monthly telephone groups/conference calls. Now get this: no one else in the company knew about this approach or cared that it disappeared when the implementer retired! But that kind of integration and convergence—of qualitative and quantitative, real and virtual—is what I think the future should bring.

WALKOWSKI So, how would you suggest "more sizzle" be added to bulletin boards?

BÉLISLE I think that bulletin board groups go against the grain of contemporary research: do it now, do it quickly, make the decision, move on. Bulletin boards (like this one) are great to explore issues, something that qualitative research, as recently practiced, has not been doing. Maybe they need to be positioned differently: exploratory research, issues research, development research, strategy development—anything but marketing research!

SWEET I am only going to address real-time and bulletin boards as I do not use listserv/e-mail discussions. Personally, I am not sure I have a preference. It's sort of like food—sometimes I like lobster (a slow and steady meal) and sometimes turkey (a quick and easy meal). It depends on the holiday! Moderating bulletin boards is slow and steady and more time-consuming, whereas chat rooms are quick but require great focus, keyboard dexterity, ability to multi-process, and a willingness to be under great stress and handle technical or other problems with calm. As a moderator, I like both online types and also like doing in-person groups. Selecting the best online (or offline) methodology depends on the project and objectives. It is usually clear to me when chat rooms or bulletin boards are superior to in-person groups (or each other). I see them as other research tools with their own set of benefits and shortcomings, but they can be superior in reaching busy, geographically dispersed respondents. My take is that respondents like both chat rooms and bulletin boards, and I hear this from them constantly. They like being involved in what they consider cutting edge. I think their preference is more related to their involvement and interest in the subject than the methodology. I have talked with women about shopping in real-time online chats, bulletin boards, and in-person, and they love it all ways because they are highly involved in the subject.

ZINCHIAK My experience with bulletin boards is limited. From what I have seen, the depth of information can be greater. While real-time groups are good for many situations, I feel the same as Pierre [Bélisle] and David [Van Nuys]—that you see a lot of one-line answers; respondents don't always take as much time to truly think about their responses. The probing involved in real-time groups does not always produce what you need because you can't always take all the time needed without sacrificing other parts of the discussion. I have found some clients want to include more in an online discussion guide than they would for a traditional group. Perhaps their perception is that real-time groups move much faster than traditional so they feel they can fit more in. Some clients have much higher expectations for real-time chat groups than traditional groups. I think it will be easier to manage client expectations with bulletin boards. I also think respondents will be easier to manage over the course of the board and probing will be much more involved. A final comment here. I see question composition very differently between real-time and bulletin boards. Longer questions with more of an introduction give fewer opportunities to be misinterpreted and imply more of a commitment on the respondent's part to answer in-depth. In addition, respondents have more time to think and compose a response.

VAN NUYS Monica [Zinchiak]'s remarks about clients expecting to pack more guide content into chat groups strike home for me inasmuch as I am going to be conducting five chat groups over the next couple of days. I think the guide is much too long and detailed. I've tried to impress the client with this but she has other people she has to answer to. So, I think they will have to see that it is a problem in the first group and then they will be more willing to make adjustments for the remaining four. But I don't like the possibility that it will make the technique look less useful than they were expecting.

SWEET One way I manage this (because they are already stressful enough) is to tell the client that my experience is that they can have forty to fifty preset questions with some room for follow-up probes. How did I arrive at this number? Well, my varied past started in accounting so I counted from the transcripts. I realized it was safe to estimate an average of two minutes a question and have probing room.

HERBERT My experience is limited to online focus groups. I'm interested in them from the point of view of qualitative research and what they have to offer in this process. I certainly do not see them replacing face-to-face groups; they do not have the richness of response because of the lack of all the face-to-face cues. On the other hand, it is real social interaction taking place in real time, and in my experience respondents feel involved with the other people in the group rather than simply the information stream. How online groups are moderated is also very important in either raising or lowering the level of involvement respondents feel. We often use two moderators working together, although only one types at a time while the other one helps to follow the process. Online groups require a very high level of concentration on the part of the moderators if they are to achieve a high level of involvement for the respondents. It is not something you can do while doing anything else. Your concentration has to be absolute. There is no doubt that it is a bit chaotic and takes some time to get used to the social rhythm of an online group, but I would suggest that there is a real social rhythm. The other thing that fascinates me about online groups is the light they can shed on "electronic interactivity." What is going on with people who are removed from geographical and time constraints, who are not able to see, hear, or smell each other, and yet are able to interact with one another in real time? Given the increasing part communicating and interacting electronically is going to play in the future, I find it fascinating to get at what is happening. Online groups represent the first early steps of electronic interactivity in what will be seen in the future as rather primitive chat-room technology. It feels very exciting to be at the edge of trying to understand this, and it is one of the key reasons why I conducted the comparative study that I referred to in my introductory remarks.

WINTER I can only address the issue of online focus groups (chat) because that's the only medium I have used to date (around seventy-five groups). However, while I agree that many respondent answers lack the depth found in traditional groups, that isn't always true. It is very much a function of the topic and respondent segment. And, while it is natural to compare online groups to traditional, they are, in fact, a different animal. Michael [Herbert] made some interesting observations about the "social rhythm" of real-time online groups. I have found a very different set of dynamics that happens in an online group—and "rhythm" is a term I've often used. If the topic is right, I have found the experience, as a moderator, downright exhilarating. I'm wondering if the way to encourage the use of bulletin boards is to position them as a brand new method of qualitative exploration.

VAN NUYS I have a different hypothesis as to why bulletin board groups are a harder sell to clients. I think real-time chat is seen as technologically sexier, whereas bulletin boards have been around for a long time and smack of old technology.

BÉLISLE Interesting issue. They may be seen as sexier because the kids use them all the time. My sixteen-year-old daughter chats, listens to MP3s, talks on the phone, does homework, and watches TV—all at the same time. But I recall that CompuServe had chat rooms (they called them "conference rooms"), so I'm not sure that bulletin boards preceded real-time chats by that much.

SWEET I sit around roaring with laughter about what respondents say. I feel close to the respondents. Maybe it is like blind people whose other senses jump in to compensate, and though the experience is different from in-person, it is still rich with the intensity of the other devoted senses. My husband actually believes that doing online groups satisfies my need for drama and adrenalin and minimizes my need to dramatize around the house. (Hey, it's a lay point of view from someone who should know.) Maybe I am happier that I am not traveling as much, since business travel wears me down. Whatever the reasons, I love the excitement and thrill of real-time online groups, the peaceful thoughtfulness of bulletin boards, and the kinesthetic experience of in-person work.

SABENA Actually, I like both real-time chats and bulletin board groups. I have found them both to be amazingly rich if I layer the questions well and keep injecting probes and comments the way I would in a real-time group. Frankly, I love the ability to spawn the pre-loaded questions and to follow the dialogue in both formats. I love the feeling of injecting probes that show I was paying attention to who said what earlier (just like in face-to-face groups). I find that each group has a personality all its own, just like face-to-face groups. I like bulletin board groups because the questions can be sent out at midnight and people can respond at their leisure. I have been amazed at their candor and faithfulness. My bulletin board group included thirty-one people who wrote very personal and emotional things and stayed with me all week. My clients liked the bulletin board group the best because of the richness of the data. Clients have not been pleased with the show rate in some of the real-time studies, however, which has been my biggest problem. At least one or two have been very turned off to the chat room methodology because our show rate was so poor. The data was great, just not enough bodies (three or four instead of the eight I had promised). We over-recruited plenty, paid them, and called them, but it was a problem. Things have improved a lot since then. My last six chat rooms were well attended and went exceedingly well. For most things, I think respondents prefer the ninety-minute format. For something they're truly engaged in (such as a chronic disease state), the week-long bulletin board gives them a community of people. They want to exchange e-mail addresses with each other because they've really come to know each other during the week of sharing confidences.

WALKOWSKI To what do you attribute the lower show rates for online groups?

BÉLISLE A number of things, I surmise. First, there is often not a live, talking, human recruiter. Am I saying that a spoken word is more binding than one written? Perhaps. Also, going online doesn't really require a rearrangement of time or a commitment of resources. I suspect that without that commitment, rendezvous are a lot easier to break. Finally, if you don't show, you're not disappointing a live person but an online avatar. [**Read more about recruitment issues in qualitative research online in the "Tricks of the Trade" section.**]

3.4 Validation Issues

WALKOWSKI As far as I can tell, there seems to be a dearth of published side-by-side comparisons of online and offline qualitative research studies. In your opinion, how important is it to conduct these side-by-side comparisons?

BÉLISLE I recently conducted side-by-side research for two companies that had a profound impact on the clients' perceptions of online research, my own confidence in online findings, and my renewed belief in the value of multiple lines of inquiry on any given project. So, yes: as with any new technique, particularly one that seems threatening to many, side-by-side studies can be really important in changing attitudes.

SABENA Actually I think it's our own responsibility to be doing this research on research if we hope to sell online studies to our clients. I just participated in a side-by-side comparison of face-to-face, chat room, and bulletin board with the same moderator (me), screener, and discussion guide. The results were so encouraging we're presenting them at an upcoming conference.

VAN NUYS I think the side-by-side studies are very important, even the anecdotal ones such as we are hearing about in discussions such as this. The question as to the validity of these new techniques immediately comes to mind for researcher and client alike. It is certainly something that I have wondered about. The early returns, reported by some of the discussants here and by others elsewhere, are reassuring to me, and they give me some ammunition with which to approach my clients. I don't demand that the comparative studies be done by academics. I'm supposedly an academic myself, so I have some right to be suspicious. I don't think we are doing science, as qualitative practitioners. I think a lot of what we do is art, intuition, and craft. We can learn from other craftsmen, as we hear about their comparative experiences.

BÉLISLE You're right. As practitioners, we're looking for relative comfort with new methodologies, not absolute proof one way or the other.

LOVEJOY I've seen numerous attempts to conduct formal academic-style comparisons of different qualitative methodologies, and I remain enormously skeptical that this gives better insight than less formal evaluations. There are just too many variables. I think it's important that qualitative researchers experiment with different methodologies and decide for themselves what works best for them in terms of achieving different types of objectives. For example, Michael [Herbert] and I have come to some significantly different conclusions about the role and value of chat groups. Could some formal study tell us that one of us is right and the other wrong? I don't believe so. It's not something someone else can tell you, it's something you need to try for yourself. Can we assist that learning process by sharing experiences? Absolutely. But I don't believe there is any one true answer.

BÉLISLE It's quite true that comparing qualitative methodologies is like counting water. Anyone predisposed to doubt the results will not, I suspect, be convinced by these attempts. I recall listening to a presentation from researchers who had compared a face-to-face and chat methodology. I remember being unimpressed with the rigor they had brought to the exercise, and the superficiality of their observations. What I would take from Ben [Lovejoy]'s point is that these side-by-side comparisons should be for the consumption of the researcher and their clients primarily, rather than an attempt at public conversion.

ZINCHIAK I agree with everything my colleagues have said. I would add that the best side-by-side comparisons will be those evaluated and reported by the client sector, evaluating results and determining whether the same decisions will be made. This will best serve all parties—researchers, academics, and buyers of research. I think that clients are looking to us to conduct these comparisons though, which is sort of a Catch-22.

SWEET The words Monica [Zinchiak] says also come from my mouth. I think everyone is looking to someone else for the side-by-side work. What concerns me is the design of these types of studies and the interpretations. I like Monica's thought about somehow judging based on action items or decisions. When someone tells me they asked the exact same questions in all three venues it is hard for me to believe, and sometimes I question whether a project can legitimately be done in all three mediums. Some of the points of comparison can be strange, such as number of words by venue used as an indicator of effectiveness.

BÉLISLE Although I didn't use word counts as the key metric in the work I did, I looked at word counts because it was so easily available. The results weren't at all different from what you'd expect: many more words in a bulletin board session, shorter sentences in a chat, et cetera.

HERBERT I think it is critical for the research industry to conduct these side-by-side comparisons. Further, it is critical that there is some degree of consistency at least in terms of the substantive content of the discussion between the three different methodologies or else how would we know whether the responses (and therefore the conclusions and recommendations drawn) are a result of the chosen methodology rather than a result of the research findings? In qualitative research we are using the philosophical and epistemological underpinnings of social science. Hence the use of terms such as research objectives, methodology, research findings, and conclusions. In turn, the social science framework is based on the natural science underpinnings. The philosophy of social science addresses the philosophical and research issues and differences between conducting natural and social science. This is well-trodden and well-understood territory, and I raise it not to be highfalutin or academic but because it is essential for us to understand the status and validity of our qualitative research findings. Consequently, we need to calibrate, as far as possible, the difference in findings which are attributed to any of the different methodological variables of a qualitative study.

WALKOWSKI What anecdotal evidence do you have that sheds light on the comparability of online and offline qualitative methodologies?

BÉLISLE As I indicated above, I conducted and presented a paper on a case study that used chat, bulletin boards, and face-to-face methods: similar respondent profiles, similar guides, one analyst. The approach taken was to compare the strategic implications (for each of seven study objectives) that each method alone would yield and to compare those implications. The simplest outcome, and the one I was hoping for, was that the implications would be the same. In fact, most were. But in two areas, the implications were radically different: online, the service under study was thought too expensive, while the face-to-face participants found it reasonable; online, the value-added of the sponsoring organization was very positive, while face-to-face participants were much more negative. It was only after playing around with these findings for a while that I concluded, to my satisfaction, that all findings were correct, and depended on the context of the questioning. In short, trying to compare the approaches was the wrong question. My conclusion and new mantra is that we have to embrace the concept of multiple lines of inquiry if we are to get more complete (truer) answers.

ZINCHIAK In 1999 a client hired me for a series of real-time groups that built upon each other. I think we completed ten total. After all the findings were reported, he disclosed to me that they had conducted traditional groups with the same objectives and goals. In essence, he was doing his own validation of the online methodology. He was pleased, as the results were nearly identical.

HERBERT As I mentioned in my introduction, we have conducted a comparative study of online and face-to-face qualitative group discussions using the same respondents for each. It was conducted across four life stages: teenagers, younger singles and couples without kids, families, and over fifties. It was conducted in Australia and Canada using two substantive and different topics. Everything that could be rotated was (for example, whether the respondents did face-to-face or online first, and which topic of the two they did first). A total of sixteen groups were conducted, eight face-to-face and eight online. We had all respondents fill in a questionnaire after each of the research experiences, and after completing both the face-to-face and online, they filled in a third questionnaire comparing the two processes and their experience of them. Much of this is still to be written up, but fundamentally, in terms of substantive content, there is no greater difference in findings between face-to-face and online than there would be between two different face-to-face groups. This is different than commenting on the richness of the data, or the length of responses, where indeed there are differences, as many others have already noted. In terms of respondent preferences across the four life stages, the majority did not prefer one style but had found each interesting in its own right. Teenagers preferred online to face-to-face but none of the other three life-stage groups had an online preference over face-to-face.

SABENA The side-by-side study I conducted two months ago on a chronic disease state showed absolutely no difference in emotional affect, depth of content, disclosure of personal information, or degree of group bonding from face-to-face to chat room to bulletin board venues. The only difference was that I probably got more disabled types in the chat room and bulletin board, and recruiting was easier and less expensive in the online environment.

WALKOWSKI **Have you conducted any online qualitative studies that probably would not have been conducted at all if online qualitative capabilities were not available?**

LOVEJOY The most obvious one is where the sample is scattered geographically and the budget isn't there to make offline research an option. We've run one project where respondents were in about seven or eight different countries, for example. However, I would say that in those circumstances a telephone conference call should be considered alongside online methodologies.

BÉLISLE I conducted a bulletin board study for an organization that was interested in understanding what attracted heavy users of specialty products to these products. Because these respondents comprise an infinitesimal part of the population, I believe it unlikely that they could have been brought together as a temporary community except online, by recruitment from an online panel. It would have been possible to conduct a one-shot survey through a mail panel, but the interaction between participants was only possible in an online setting. I conducted another study that involved the reactions of allergy sufferers to a Web site design. That study would have been very difficult to conduct offline because of the small numbers involved (quotas of allergy types and medications). More importantly, though, I believe that the results of an offline study would have failed to capture two key issues of crucial importance to the implications. First, by making participants totally anonymous, we concentrated on the words they were writing (the way their lives were run by their allergies) rather than on the sometimes humorous appearance an allergy sufferer can exhibit (to non-sufferers, of course!). Second, by bringing together (in a chat room) allergy sufferers from across the continent, the researcher and observers were able to witness how allergy symptoms (while different, and attributable to different triggers in different parts of the continent) had the common effect of severely restricting the options of the sufferers. In other words: we could have conducted a study offline, but it would not have been this study, and it would have likely resulted in different findings and different implications.

WINTER Three types of studies come to mind. The first has to do with the turnaround issue. Given that the research question was appropriate to online, we were able to recruit and complete the groups within a time frame that we simply could not have done with traditional groups. Another type of situation where online has been the answer is when we can't get to all geographic areas. We typically go to three areas of the United States for traditional groups, but there are times when either timing or client travel restrictions prevent us from doing so. In these cases, we may use online to fill the geographical gaps. Finally, we recently conducted what we fondly refer to as the "icky disease" study. The subject had to do with a condition that affects relatively few people (the client provided a list) and involves sensitive issues. The information we obtained was incredibly rich as these folks were very forthcoming online, knowing that someone was interested in listening to their problems. Perhaps we could have done this by phone, but I think people had one more level of anonymity by participating online.

ZINCHIAK Last month I did some online groups. It was an ad test for a highly targeted magazine. The client's budget would not accommodate travel, but more importantly, the highly targeted segment wouldn't come together easily city-to-city for two main reasons—low incidence and the magazine topic was highly controversial (people would not want to admit that they participate in this activity). My client would not have conducted qualitative research any other way.

SWEET I have done a number of them. Often it is because the audience is geographically dispersed and/or low incidence. I bet if I looked back that I would find that 80 percent (maybe more) could not be done in-person.

SABENA One was among U.S. customers of a Swedish company. There were only eighteen customers in the United States to recruit from, so we could never have done a single group, and I certainly wouldn't have traveled to fourteen different states to do one-on-ones. It could have been done through telephone interviews, but then they couldn't have reacted to the Web site materials. Another study involved inputting personal data into a retirement planning Web site to watch the numbers and graphs shift. While we could have done this in an in-person usability lab, it would have been much more expensive and not as true-to-life as the way this Web site was intended to be used. Also, with financial data, respondents might have been loathe to do that in front of others in the same room.

HERBERT I agree with everyone that online allows budgets to go further, especially when it provides the option for saving on international travel budgets. I have been involved in using a mix of face-to-face and online groups in the United Kingdom while conducting online groups in other countries to save on travel expenses on several projects.

VAN NUYS As others have suggested, the thing that comes most readily to mind is the ability of online to overcome the geographical separation of sparsely distributed respondents, as well as different countries. For example, I did online chat Web site usability testing among IT personnel in five countries for a major workstation manufacturer. In another study, I held chats with Web master affiliates of an online dating portal. There would not have been enough of these in any given city to conduct a face-to-face group. In other projects, clients have wanted to get a feel for a national sample but had a budget for only one or two groups. No way that could have been done except online.

3.5 Online Moderation Skills

WALKOWSKI In what ways is moderating online the same as moderating offline?

VAN NUYS Both require an ability to listen between the lines, to be curious, to play dumb to a certain extent, to be playful and humorous, to keep in mind what the client needs to hear, to treat respondents with respect, and to think on your feet.

SABENA Both require you to pay attention and to circle back to things people said (or wrote) earlier so they know you care and are paying attention. In fact, during one online group I had a big fight with my husband. He was standing at the entrance to my office (a few feet from our bedroom) screaming at me about something. My attention was understandably distracted. My clients noticed I was interacting less actively with the participants and sent me an e-mail about it. I was sending the pre-loaded questions in, but not probing individual respondents by name as I usually do. It made a big difference in the tonality of the group. As soon as I went back to probing, the group went deeper into the material. (You'll be relieved to know that my husband and I patched it up between us later.)

HERBERT In both situations first you are wanting everyone to feel socially comfortable and free to express themselves and wanting to give something of themselves and to get involved. In order to do this you have to give something of yourself and show that you are involved and also that you find what they are saying very interesting. It seems to me you have to establish this level of rapport quickly with respondents whether it is online or offline. In both face-to-face and online chat you are selecting and shaping the areas of discussion you want to pursue while keeping everyone involved. This always takes some doing and is more difficult online because online discussions are more difficult to follow. This is exactly why we often use two moderators as I've mentioned before.

WINTER Most of the same techniques convert. Listening becomes reading. Perhaps the ability to digest things quickly also carries over from one medium to the other. I've always felt that intuitiveness is a talent possessed by the really good moderators. That is certainly necessary with online focus groups, but a little harder to employ without seeing respondents. However, the ability to recognize when respondents need encouragement or recognition (perhaps to quiet them) is as important online as offline.

WALKOWSKI In what ways is moderating online different from moderating offline?

BÉLISLE The differences are due to the different characteristics of the universe. Online is mediated through writing, with no physical proximity and no observation between participants and moderator. Offline (I exclude telephone, not having done any of those interviews) is the converse. That means [in online groups]:

- responses can be more extreme (no threat of physical hurt, complete anonymity, writing can reveal more than talking);
- there is more danger of the group blowing up; so interventions must be carefully gauged;
- modulation of content/meaning via body language is not possible; therefore, all modulation has to be achieved through the content stream, which includes a limited number of emoticons and acronyms. Therefore, the moderator has to be very quick on his/her feet (make that hands, haha) and literate.

ZINCHIAK Adding to Pierre [Bélisle]'s list: Crafting the moderator's guide requires a slightly different approach. In an offline group, my guide is written for the clients to follow along. I use the areas in the discussion guide, but I follow the questions loosely—not verbatim. In online groups you have to pay careful attention to how those questions will be written and interpreted. Back-peddling or correcting yourself (because a question wasn't interpreted correctly or doesn't flow the way you would like) is sometimes time consuming and awkward. I find I rely more on the transcripts with online groups for analysis. This may be due to the convenience of getting them immediately. I think it may have more to do with the speed in which the group moves. Also, I have more of a lasting memory or impression when I have conducted a live group. More of my senses have been touched and I have a stronger impression.

BÉLISLE Good point. I caught myself, once, the day before an online group, without a guide! Face-to-face guides are, for me, often vague affairs to be filled in on the spot. By contrast, a question in an online guide is almost like (well, it is, actually) an open-ended question in a questionnaire.

SABENA Monica [Zinchiak], I so agree with your comments on the moderator's guide and the transcripts. The online questions have to be carefully crafted and layered to maximize each response. I also have less sense of the findings after the online group until I read the transcript. Things moved so fast during the group that I didn't get the clear-cut impressions and conclusions I get during a face-to-face group.

VAN NUYS I'll answer this in terms of chat, which is the modality I am most experienced with. Moderating chat requires an ability to phrase questions and probes much more succinctly than face-to-face. It also requires a certain talent for knowing how what is typed will be read. Not everyone has that ability to step outside of his or her own writing and quickly assess the impact objectively. As has been mentioned, it certainly requires being a fluent and speedy typist (or employing one during the session). It also requires speed reading to keep up with the flow. It demands a certain comfort level with the challenges of technology. It helps to have had some experience with other forms of chat, so that one is familiar with how to project personality, convey humor, and use emoticons. It definitely requires the setting of appropriate client expectations for what the medium can and cannot do. It requires a good intuitive sense, an ability to read between the lines.

SABENA Well, certainly there's an absence of those first physical impressions you get from people. In some ways this means that visual cues and prejudices are avoided. Some moderators miss all the overt warmth of face-to-face. There's no body language to fall back on.

SWEET Besides all the missing visual and verbal cues, some of the other factors that make online moderating and analysis different are:

- less domination to manage
- less gender influence to manage
- transparent and easy client communication
- long-winded stories do not take precious group time
- can be conducted on the road while doing other projects
- requires decent keyboard skills (or a hired keyboarder)
- cannot use some techniques effectively (collage)
- security issues can prevent some subjects from being covered
- no respondent interruption
- instant transcripts

HERBERT Besides the differences already mentioned, I find the most major one is following the respondent responses in relation to what question or issue they are commenting on. This takes a lot of concentration and adapting to the different social interactional rhythm of an online group compared with a face-to-face group. I need that rhythm for the group to work whether online or offline.

WINTER As I suggested above, one may have to digest things a bit faster than with a traditional group. The phrasing of questions is also different. It took me a while to realize that I could use compound questions in the online groups that helped make the flow smoother and less stilted. I might not do so in traditional groups because I can personally address individual situations and be a lot less restricted to the actual order of the guide. The online moderating experience, in my case, is much more structured than with traditional groups.

WALKOWSKI What differences are there in moderating a real-time chat versus a message board discussion versus a listserv (MEG—Moderated E-mail Group) discussion? (Even if you have no experience with a particular mode of online qualitative, offer your expectations of the differences among them.)

BÉLISLE I imagine a listserv discussion as a series of parallel one-on-ones, accreting with new material at each iteration. I can't imagine why I would use such a mode, or under what circumstances. The differences between chat and bulletin boards are clearer to me. The chat is real time and the bulletin board is not—their differences stem from that characteristic. The chat is more intense and subject to the vagaries of real-time Internet like latency, slow connections, drop-offs, and server issues. Ultimately, though, the process is driven by the "river of text" (just made that up) on which the words flow by. This river only flows one way, so that there is little chance to explore side-currents (ooh, I'm getting poetic!) before it's time to regain the main channel. That characteristic determines how questions are worded, what topics are best handled in a chat, and how much depth should be expected. By contrast, the bulletin board session is timeless and can deal with more profound issues that require more reflection, introspection, homework, and memories. It is almost not mediated since the questions have to stand on their own, without clarification, for some time. Those characteristics also determine how to format questions and what topics can be appropriate for them.

ZINCHIAK Adding to the list: You will spend more time moderating a bulletin board than a real-time group. Real-time groups have a finite period of time just as with a traditional face-to-face group. With bulletin boards, you have the flexibility of using as much time as you need to read postings, ponder them, and create more probes. Also, generally there are more respondents in bulletin board groups and this will require more time to read and probe.

Though my experience is very limited with bulletin boards, I can see a difference in that there could be more opportunities to conduct exercises or give respondents daily assignments and have them come back and report to you. In a real-time group you would have to assign before the group date and time, or they may forget some of their assignment experience. With bulletin boards, they could do the task at their convenience, sit right down at the computer, and tell you about it while it is still fresh in their minds.

SABENA At least some of the bulletin board flows by itself with less attention from the moderator, and respondents write incredibly detailed responses. They jump right into the questions that I know are going to come up later as if they can't wait to divulge.

WALKOWSKI If an experienced offline moderator asked you, "How can I tell if online qualitative is something I'd be good at?" or "How do I determine if online moderating is right for me?" how would you respond?

BÉLISLE I'd say, "Try it." But that's probably not the answer you're looking for. I think I'd try to find out whether the moderator is a "touchy-feely" type. Does the moderator like analysis and report-writing or the "performance" part of offline work? Does the moderator spend resources only on improving moderation skills or on other areas like analysis? How does the moderator feel about computers and the Web? How comfortable is he/she with his/her current practice? How good is he/she at typing? Does he/she belong to any chat or bulletin board groups? And I suppose, ultimately, is the current client set likely to be served by online work?

ZINCHIAK Interest and curiosity are your best gauges about whether they will like it. Of course some basic typing skills and comfort using the technology are important. Something that I believe helped me feel comfortable was playing around with bulletin boards and chat rooms on AOL in the mid-nineties. I developed a rhythm and language that at that time was unique. The language and culture of the Internet chat room is no longer just for the young, computer savvy, or rich. I agree with Pierre [Bélisle]—try one, observe one, do a demo, create one with your friends or colleagues, go to a public chat room somewhere and participate in the discussion, or volunteer for a spot as a bulletin board or chat room leader. If you get turned on by the fast-paced playfulness, and can direct them, you will be good.

VAN NUYS I'd have to echo what Pierre [Bélisle] and Monica [Zinchiak] have said. That is, try one. Follow your interest. I should add, however, that my experiences with AOL-type chat rooms and IRC have mostly been a turnoff for me. They are much too glib and smarmy for my taste. A bit too much posturing. I think a lot of the participants are quite young and so there is a juvenile flavor to a lot of those public rooms. Also, a lot of the language is a bit raw for my taste. So what I'm saying is that I think a person might be turned off by general Internet chat but would probably take to the more purposefully structured version that we embrace.

SABENA If they're asking, they're probably going to like it. If you shudder at the thought of it, you're probably too techno-phobic and hidebound to try something different. That sounds judgmental, but it's really a willingness to experiment.

SWEET I'd describe the experience of both and ask them if that appeals to them. I'd go into all the pros and cons—exhilarating, stressful (clients sending notes, two people on the phone, respondents asking for clarification, and system crashes), unexpected situations to deal with, office lights off five minutes after group, no travel, desire to multi-process and really think by the seat of your pants for changes that occur. I'd tell them what my best and worst group looks like. They usually know whether it appeals to them. I just met someone today. I asked her if she was competitive and if she liked sports and other adrenalin-producing activities. She immediately agreed. That's for chat. For bulletin boards I say it is a long steady session that you can put in from two to eight or more hours a day, especially in the beginning with larger groups and involved subjects. I think it is an easier place to transfer skills and step into the online arena without the overwhelming stress possible with chats.

3.6 Tricks of the Trade

WALKOWSKI What advice do you have about the recruitment process to maximize show rates?

SWEET With online make sure that you, the moderator, know exactly how they are recruiting from beginning to end and see every confirmation document. Initially, when I was assured that recruiting was done with attention to all the details, I did not realize that some of the recruiters have never even been near professional facility recruiters and had no idea what the established procedures were, or the high standards that had been set. I know many moderators who have had a bad experience with recruitment for online groups. And I know a few clients that were very turned off to the online methodology because of recruitment issues; some of their conclusions were that online is unreliable, it lacks credibility in reaching respondents, and questionable people are recruited. But I veer off from the main question. Suffice it to say, there's recruiting naiveté in the online arena. The good news is that it is getting better. I recommend that at least one contact with respondents be over the phone. Also, I have done pure phone recruiting with professionals and have had a very high show rate—eight or nine showed with ten recruited for members from a large association. Speed is one of the advantages of online, but whenever possible I try not to rush the recruit. I try to have one and a half or two weeks—plenty of time to select, invite, confirm, and replace cancellations. For bulletin boards, in the course of the invitation, I always give respondents an idea of the amount of daily time they can expect; so they know what they are agreeing to. Be sure to reiterate the time requirement in the confirmation and ask if they will be able to devote this amount of time.

VAN NUYS Casey [Sweet], I'd be curious what kind of daily time commitment you tell respondents to expect.

SWEET I have a bulletin board going right now with consumers. I told them it would be thirty to sixty minutes a day. I find that people happily spend more time when there is high interest in the topic. I think higher incentives (to offset lower-interest topics or busy people) get them there but do not necessarily motivate continued participation. Passion on a topic does motivate, and time just flies.

ZINCHIAK For real-time groups, I find that a phone call to confirm respondents works well. Spending just a couple of minutes with them on the phone can create even a small bond. It is more difficult for a respondent to blow off the group if she has spoken to someone and given her commitment. In other words, it is easy to ignore the e-mail confirmation and more uncomfortable for them not to show if they have spoken to a real person. In addition, that phone call can be used to confirm passwords, resolve technical problems, confirm the start time—some of the other items that affect show rates.

VAN NUYS For the sorts of reasons already spelled out by Casey [Sweet] and Monica [Zinchiak], all of my online groups so far have been recruited by professional recruiters. I generally over-recruit, recruiting twelve to get eight to ten. Popular wisdom has been that it is better to have small chat groups, six to eight respondents. However, my own experience is that I can easily handle ten (and sometimes more), and I have the impression that the ones with more people are more dynamic; there's a higher likelihood of having some sparkplugs in the group, IMHO.

ZINCHIAK My ideal number is ten participants. I have run fourteen in a real-time group before, but that was a bit too many to follow all the postings. And I was not able to probe adequately. On the flip side, my client liked all the interaction, and the dialogue was constantly streaming in. I had the feeling some of the participants were overwhelmed and didn't participate as they would have if the group was smaller. I wouldn't suggest that many to anyone.

HERBERT I agree with Casey [Sweet] and Monica [Zinchiak] about speaking at least once to online respondents on the phone before the group, as it gains much greater commitment from the respondent. I, as moderator, also find it reassuring. To maximize show rates we normally speak to respondents twice on the phone after they have been recruited. The first time we confirm their attendance, times, and passwords and ask them to visit the room at least three days before the session to make sure they are able to get in and that everything is working. Once we have established this we also call them on the day of the group to confirm that they are still able to attend and that everything is okay on their end. We find it essential to have a phone number they can be reached on while they are actually online.

BÉLISLE Consider over-recruiting and paying a partial amount to those turned away (rather than nothing or the entire stipend). In other words, recruit fifteen for eight to show, and specify in the invitation that "those selected for the session will receive X dollars." When turning away participants (I always ask for volunteers; I just won't turn anyone away arbitrarily), offer them a smaller token (say, a $20 online certificate). They're happy, you're happy, the ones who stay are happy. The drawback, of course, is the self-selection bias it introduces.

SABENA Telephone confirmation at least one time, having the telephone number of the person recruited for a last-resort reminder call, paying all who come into the waiting room (so they come back again some time), and stressing (IN CAPS IF NECESSARY) what time zone the group is scheduled for. Early recruiting was really poor and turned off a lot of clients. It's a shame because it turned some of the early triers into naysayers. I do think recruiting is getting better, however. You have to shop around to find those you trust.

WINTER For our real-time groups, we do our own recruiting and start with an e-mail invitation to a specific list of opt-in folks to our survey (screener) site. After selecting the qualified group, we follow up by phone, generally about twenty for the twelve we will finally recruit, for six to show. We do this as much for security as for show rate. We know that while it's very easy and cool to participate in an online group, the respondent has not made the same commitment as to going to a central location, and therefore is much more easily distracted and more likely to fail to show. The phone, of course, drives up the recruiting cost, but we have found the total recruitment cost to be about the same as for traditional groups.

WALKOWSKI How can an online moderator promote interaction among respondents in an online session?

SWEET One technique is to set up a debate where half the people are assigned the pros and half the cons and get them to promote their point of view. They become a team and build on each other. I have them state their positions in separate questions. Then I put them back together and give them a question to debate, taking positions against one another. And, lastly, if called for, I have them switch positions and argue the opposite. It can be lots of fun for them as they are free to speak without much of the emotional impact of disagreement, and it is harder for them to misinterpret the disagreement as a personal judgment.

VAN NUYS In real-time chat groups, the addition of some humor, either by me or respondents, seems to increase the likelihood that they will start responding to one another. The other thing that I do is probably something we all do in face-to-face groups, which is to make reference to a respondent's contribution. ("Tom says this product would take too much time to use. What do the rest of you say?") I think this increases the probability that others may address Tom directly. Beyond this, part of the initial instructions to the group might be something along these lines: "In addition to responding to my questions, I'd really like this to be a group interaction. So please feel free to address and respond to one another by name." My actual experience, as I think about it, is that I don't push for a lot of group interaction. In my experience, some online chat groups seem to be interactive spontaneously and others aren't. There is usually sufficient pressure to get through all the questions on the guide that there is not a lot of space to try to stimulate additional interactive conversation.

HERBERT I think you have to be more highly colored and flavored as a moderator in real-time chat compared with face-to-face groups. This generally causes respondents to become more involved and to "sit up and listen." In other words, you have to be more provocative as a moderator in chat than when doing face-to-face. So I'll ask things such as, "Jane has just said so and so and that seems to be the total opposite of what you were just saying, Sharon. So what do you think of what Jane is saying, Sharon?" This usually helps get people going more. Also the use of humor and banter usually livens things up—and in chat it is important to keep everyone involved and attentive. Having them not quite sure what you're going to say to them next usually makes for more lively sessions. Of course you have to be careful to steer the delicate balance between being provocative, challenging, and forthright while letting everyone know that you are encouraging them to say exactly what they want to and that you are supporting them in this.

SABENA I agree, Michael [Herbert], that you can and should take even more risks in being provocative online, using the usual humor but being a little more challenging than you might be in person. In in-person groups you could soften it with tonality or a hand on the arm (if you're female, and you're sitting near the respondent), but you don't get to do that online. It's a matter of developing a knack for "naming" the emotion that seems to be surfacing in the group, and then getting respondents to react even further. Of course, there's also a responsibility to "do no harm" in all of this, so it's a fine line. This is another reason why experienced qualitative researchers should be the only ones doing this.

BÉLISLE Truth be told, I'm not sold on the idea of promoting interaction among participants in a chat session. Participants already seem primed to take side trips in their discussions, too often on topics not related to the discussion. Those who want to bounce off comments of others already do so. As far as boards are concerned, I think that the nothing-shows-until-you've-entered-your-response is one way to "demote" interaction. I was part of a bulletin board panel last week where the moderator decided (or had to, because of the system) to use this approach every day, for every question. Needless to say, interaction was minimal. There are, of course, interventions that can promote interaction ("Everyone, Jamie said X, what do you think?"). I think, though, that (and we probably need research here!) the level of interaction is more a function of other dimensions: the length of the board, the average frequency of visits, the ability to navigate the board and view new posts. I can also see, however, where it might be possible to throw in a contentious question at the outset of the discussion to foster replies and rebuttals. This adds some risk to the project, I might add.

ZINCHIAK The nothing-shows-until-you-post method can be very effective for the initial question or two. For example, on the first couple days for this bulletin board, I logged in later in the day, and everything I wanted to say had already been posted by my esteemed colleagues. This left me feeling that I had nothing to add, except for maybe, "I agree." I could see respondents feeling a bit intimidated or left out if they can't add something original or new to the discussion. Unless they can jump in and be first on the board that day, why would they make an effort to come back and read every day if they feel that they won't have something of value to add?

SABENA In both real-time chats and bulletin boards, one important technique is calling on or probing respondents by name from time to time to encourage them to amplify something further. This gives a less robotic feeling to the pre-loaded questions. Also, in the warm-up/directions section at the beginning of each group, it is good to encourage respondents to piggyback on each other's responses just like they would in a live conversation.

WALKOWSKI What types of questions or techniques work well online?

SWEET Sentence completions, debating, pre/during/post assignments, laddering (more for bulletin boards), audits of pantries, or any area where I want to know exactly what was purchased. I'm sure there are many more. I am experimenting all the time.

ZINCHIAK I agree with Casey [Sweet]. I use sentence completion and fill in the blank. It functions as a springboard for some respondents who just don't get it. I have always liked that technique both online and offline. I have heard of collages being done in online focus groups. Respondents were sent a digital camera and software before the group. They were asked to create a collage of photos from their day-to-day life and send their collages to the moderator prior to the group. The moderator shows the collages on the white board during the group for discussion. I was told it went fabulous. What a huge commitment on the respondents' part. I believe that the digital camera was their incentive for participation. I would try this.

VAN NUYS Great ideas here from Casey [Sweet] and Monica [Zinchiak]. In addition to the sentence completion that has been mentioned, I have used animal metaphors: "If this product/service were an animal, what would it be?" This works extremely well in the online environment. Most of the questions, in my experience, are straightforward questions of the sort that you would ask in a face-to-face group.

HERBERT I agree that sentence completion works well in online chat as does word association. I've also found brand personification works well and is usually fun: "If this brand came to life as a person describe this person to me." I've also used the car and animal metaphors. I think these techniques work well both online and offline because they are easy for respondents to do and understand, and it is interesting to other respondents, especially online, as it gives all of them a chance to understand each other better, particularly as they are being denied all the physical cues.

SABENA I like numbering the questions, and asking respondents to reply to the question by number. That helps me keep track of how much we've covered and to move on appropriately. It also helps to know what's going on when a respondent's post comes after another question has been asked. I also like to layer the questions more thoroughly than I would ever do in the spoken word. For example, in one single question, I might ask: "Tell me about X. How often do you do it? What do you like about it? What don't you like about it?" This prompts respondents to write a whole paragraph of stuff before comparing what others wrote. It also avoids monosyllabic answers and wasted time.

BÉLISLE I like your idea of numbering questions. I wonder if you could train participants to always preface their answers with a number? And building on that, it might be useful not only to ask the question in the text stream, but to show it (and perhaps the one before it) in the white board. That way, everyone would always have the current questions in mind. I'm going to play with that!

WALKOWSKI What types of questions or techniques do NOT work well online? Please be sure to explain what makes them problematic.

VAN NUYS Clearly, any activity that demands real-time, physical manipulation is not going to work in an online chat. Also, although Casey [Sweet] alludes to having done it, I'm not clear how I could get people to work in pairs or trios during a chat session. Also, I don't think that long, complex questions work well in a chat session. The weighing of complex feature sets against one another is awkward in chat (though I am doing it on a project right now) because people tend to give such terse replies and it gets very time consuming if you have to keep clarifying who is responding to what.

BÉLISLE For chats, definitely, meaning-of-life questions: "How would you say the organization has been with regard to the way it treats its management echelons?" These should be left to face-to-face groups or bulletin boards. Also, I think that questions that require an evaluation by the moderator of understanding (say, of a new concept) on the part of the participant are problematic: How can I tell that you understand what this new gizmo will do unless I am in front of you watching your body language?

SABENA Any questions that lead to unexplained "yes" and "no" answers. It just slows down the group with a list of "yeses," "no's," and "sometimes," instead of the rich data you're looking for.

WALKOWSKI What other "tricks of the trade" have you learned as an online moderator?

SWEET Use ratings such as one to ten to measure strength of feeling. Check in often on bulletin boards. Address everyone by name at least once. Prepare clients to hear "it sucks" (online) rather than "it's not really the product for me" (in-person).

ZINCHIAK In real-time chats, I almost never use the browser launch feature. I do not like sending respondents away from the chat stream. Too much time can be lost in the group and I have no way of seeing how they are navigating through a Web site (if that is the exercise). Respondents move ahead of you and may lose track of time. I would prefer to show static pages in the white board and ask them where they would expect a certain area to take them (unaided) then show them this area and collect feedback.

HERBERT Monica [Zinchiak], when we use the browser we always specify that they must be back in a very specific time: "You have two minutes to look at the home page and then come back and tell us what you think." This usually works. When we haven't specified time like this, I agree, it is easy for them to wander off.

VAN NUYS It's also possible to trigger or spawn another page that tells them it's time to come back. This works fine with technical respondents, but net newbies might get a bit confused by the proliferation of windows.

HERBERT As well as asking general questions to the whole group, use individual people's names as much as possible. Keep addressing them all by name fairly often throughout the session so that you keep them involved. You have to work to concentrate hard when moderating an online group, but I agree it is really exhilarating when it works and you can feel everyone's involvement. Also, I am a great believer in introductions/warm-up in both face-to-face and online groups. It is essential that this is done thoroughly online so everyone gains a good sense of who they are in the online chat with. I always encourage them to be colorful about themselves.

VAN NUYS Michael [Herbert], what might you say to "encourage them to be colorful about themselves?"

HERBERT David [Van Nuys], the colorful thing usually comes up in the warm-up and any hint of anything colorful I will always follow up on. One time I had a respondent in a U.S. group who was in Montana and he mentioned that he was going to have a glass of Australian wine. I asked if anyone else would like one and if he could get one for each of us because we'd like to join him. I also complimented him on his choice of country for wine and asked him how he knew I was an Aussie.

ZINCHIAK I don't rely on the tech support person to greet people as they enter the waiting room. I am there, telling people who I am and answering their questions, and throwing a few things out there for conversation. If I see a new person enter, I ask everyone to say hello to the new person.

VAN NUYS In the chat group opening, I tell them there are some clients observing the interactions in a virtual back room. I suggest they wave to the clients. This gets us off to a humorous start. People respond to that invitation in different ways. I agree with Michael [Herbert] about the importance of introductions, having people get to know one another. I generally do this a bit in the waiting room, just before the group begins, asking questions about where they live, the weather there, and other light chitchat.

SWEET At the end of my introduction (welcome, no right/wrong answers, answer when/as much as you like, et cetera), I have a concluding statement: "WON OTHER THING. TYPO'S DON'T MATER. WE WALL ALL MAKKE THEM!" It breaks the ice after the dry introduction, and then I usually type, "WHEW!" I typically get lots of "lol's" and smiley faces.

BÉLISLE I have taken to asking two questions at once in chats, something like this: "Bill, how does it suck? Everyone, what were your reactions to concept number two?" This increases the chaos marvelously and loses clients totally. I'm starting to see the chat stream as the important content part of the discussion. The part of the screen that I want to train participants to look is where the important action is. So rather than typing my standard instructions in the chat stream, I'll put them up on the white board. People can read them and agree with them. Then I put the instructions away. This saves time, as well.

VAN NUYS Interesting idea, Pierre [Bélisle]. I'll have to think about that and maybe give it a try. On the other hand, having it in the chat stream helps acclimate them to how the chat stream works (text coming in from the top, for example). I suppose you argue that putting the instructions on the white board trains them for the white board, though.

BÉLISLE Six of one, half-dozen of the other, I guess. But I think that the chat stream is pretty self-evident. And if they can't get it really early on (as in the waiting room), they're just not part of the group. I've also found that this approach works well for other questions. For instance, I was doing name research, and for each name there were perhaps four questions: association, likes, dislikes, and I forget what else. Repeating the names and the questions in the text stream became very tedious. In a second project, I put the names up on the white board, and the four questions, too. This saved a lot of time without using up the text stream flow.

SABENA I think the clients need more help in all of this than the respondents. Depending on the topic, the respondents seem very voluble and involved. The clients still have glitches if they haven't been prepped well in a demo or have unreasonable expectations. I can't stress how important it is to single out respondents by name at least once in a group. I've found almost all other projective techniques work well online, but I haven't tried collage or drawings yet. Also, when the group is running a little longer than we had hoped, I throw in an encouraging line about how well the group is doing and how we're almost through, so please just hang in for a few more minutes. Online chats seem to start off a little more slowly than face-to-face groups, and close out a little later than I would normally allow in a face-to-face group. Perhaps that's because they're only ninety minutes to start with, and I'm still trying to fit in two hours of stuff. Of course, none of this is an issue in the bulletin board group.

3.7 The Future

WALKOWSKI What technological improvements must be made to push online qualitative to a higher level of acceptance in the marketing and marketing research communities?

VAN NUYS The first technological improvement is probably even more bandwidth. Even with my DSL connection, I find streaming video is a bit herky-jerky and the image can only fill up a small part of the screen real estate. Also, more respondents need to have broadband. The build-out is likely to be uneven on a global basis. So some parts of the world are likely to be unavailable for this sort of research. Video seems like the obvious next technological improvement (and, of course, the audio to go with it). I have mixed feelings about that likely development, however. As much as we decry the limitations of online text-based approaches, there are some advantages: immediate and no-cost transcripts, no interrupting, no dominating or bullying, everyone formulating their answers at the same time with less influencing of one another, and so on. I think there is room for incremental improvement of existing chat and bulletin board software. And, if these improvements happen, there will be a higher level of acceptance. As both Michael [Herbert] and Pat [Sabena] have suggested, some way of tracking how responses relate to questions on chat, using an auto-numbering scheme or such, would be a help. Graphical tools that would permit easy access to having respondents draw, collage, et cetera, would also be good. On both real-time chats and bulletin boards, it might (or might not) be good to have the capability of respondents uploading a snapshot of themselves into a special area.

HERBERT I agree with David [Van Nuys]. The big technological improvements to do with online qualitative are going to be related to much more bandwidth and therefore opening the door to video/audio communication. Pretty amazing stuff really, which returns me to some of my comments earlier about what is going on when people are communicating and interacting with each other electronically rather than face-to-face. This seems to me a whole area which needs a lot of attention paid to it and a very fruitful area for academic study. Returning a little closer to the present, we have thought about having respondent photos scanned onto the browser so that everyone could see a picture of each other. I take David's point about sometimes the need or desire for respondents to have a high degree of anonymity. We did a project on a drug education site with teenagers/young adults where we wanted them to be very honest about their drug usage and found the anonymity of online groups to be excellent for this. I'm sure photos in this instance would have been counterproductive. I've also bemoaned the need for typing in online chat. I believe there will be in the future a use for this type of exchange because of the anonymity, regardless of whatever the technological capabilities become.

BÉLISLE The usual: more robust technology, more pipe capacity, less latency, more connectivity. In a previous post, I (and others) also mentioned some of the current issues with software functionality. These issues, in my experience, go across suppliers and have to be resolved to make the experience even more painless.

SWEET I am not convinced that it is technology that is being rejected, except for the lack of visual and voice. I find the idea of online qualitative is often rejected without knowing many technology specifics. I think as the people learn of the variety of successful ways to use the technology and maybe hear that a competitor or a respected colleague used it, they will be more open. Also, it will help to have researchers themselves become more knowledgeable and able to talk about it more intelligently. Online qualitative needs many more knowledgeable advocates of its valuable and appropriate uses. I can see five to eight years from now that online venues will be accepted tools in most marketers' toolboxes. Technology will naturally move forward and be enhanced.

ZINCHIAK One of the most impactful improvements that can be made to gain acceptance is to create security measures to protect client materials. I have heard screen capture is now protected, but that doesn't stop someone from snapping a photo. I am not so sure technological improvements will help increase acceptance of this methodology in the research community. Validity of findings will do a lot more to give this methodology forward movement.

WINTER The technology improvements will happen without us pushing. The key is going to be to determine what the enhancements can do for us as researchers because online can allow us to add several dimensions to traditional research. Take the addition of real-time video, as an example. This will give us the option to capture (perhaps) body language, but there may be times when we only want to use the video for product or concept demos. I think that as the technology improves, we will have a vast array of new options.

WALKOWSKI What challenges do we face getting there?

VAN NUYS I think the challenges are mostly technological. I guess the other challenge is to our own creativity—to discover, invent new ways to use these tools, to come up with techniques that go beyond a mere interpolation of what we already do. I think the sharing we have been doing here is a step in that direction. As we share our knowledge and our own creative tricks, more of us will be out there selling them to clients, which will drive up acceptance, which will benefit us all.

HERBERT As well as the challenges brought about by changes in technology and our capacity to get our heads around them (especially non-techie types like me), I think another big challenge is building a theoretical underpinning of what is going on with people when they are interacting and communicating electronically. The whole body of knowledge of social psychology provides us with a very sound theoretical underpinning for face-to-face qualitative focus groups from a number of different angles. But it seems we know relatively little about what is the real social dynamic when people interact electronically. For example, what happens to normative behavior and group norms? If people are not under real physical scrutiny of one another, how does it affect their interaction and how they are likely to respond to different issues? Lots of questions and few answers yet.

BÉLISLE I think the current challenge is the weakness of the dot-com sector, which is where much of the push for online work came. I'd guess that we face a handful of quarters before we start getting demand back up to frenzy levels. But I do think that we're in the diffusion phase now, rather than trying to gain acceptance.

VAN NUYS I am also concerned that one spinoff of the dot-com downturn is that it may slow down or eliminate technological improvements and the emergence of hardware/software products designed to improve online research.

BÉLISLE You are absolutely right. The coming competition will be on price rather than features.

WALKOWSKI It appears that broadband connections will continue to increase. If you've not already addressed this issue above, what impact do you think this will have on the role of online qualitative?

VAN NUYS As more people get broadband, it will make our samples more and more representative of the world at large, which is a good thing. When it moves to video, something will be gained and something will be lost. When I spoke above of what would be lost, I forgot to mention the anonymity and the absence of racial, age, and social status cues. I think we've seen that there are ways in which the absence of that information is a good thing. Maybe when video arrives, we won't want to use it all the time. Maybe we will have sessions where it is on some of the time but off at others. For example, maybe we'll start groups "blind" and then go to video only after people have committed themselves on certain issues.

HERBERT It will mean video, and, as I understand it, there will be a lot of issues and problems to sort out before it can be used successfully—but one day it will come. As David [Van Nuys] and I have mentioned, I still think there will be a role for the non–face-to-face group for reasons of anonymity on sensitive subjects or subjects that compromise the law.

BÉLISLE Regardless of how it pans out in terms of our interface with participants and clients, greater penetration of broadband will increase our ability to test multimedia material more widely.

SWEET It will have a huge impact. It will make the following possible: streaming video, video or other storyboards, easy Web site review in groups, more voice capabilities, and less frustration all around.

WALKOWSKI The bottom-line question is: where do you see online qualitative headed over the next three to five years?

VAN NUYS There is no doubt in my mind that it is going to go to video. A company in Florida is already offering a virtual video capability. I think it will take off very slowly at first but ultimately is likely to become fairly standard. Here's a thought: What if voice recognition got really good, so that people didn't have to type? Then we could retain the advantages of text discussion but it would be fuller and richer. However, I think that possibility will likely be eclipsed by audio/video. It's funny, but as I think about this, I'm not quite as keen on video as I thought I would be. I guess I'm an old-fashioned guy. I like the printed word.

HERBERT The technology will get better and more powerful and IMHO this will greatly increase the use of online qualitative. I don't think it will ever replace face-to-face qualitative, but, as many have alluded to throughout this bulletin board, there will be a place for both. As online qualitative becomes more popular and pervasive, we are going to have to understand the basic nature of this type of social interaction—there I've said it again.

BÉLISLE Increasing acceptance from clients; ditto from qualitative researchers. Although we say online won't replace face-to-face, I think inevitably there will be some migration from face-to-face. We're at the dawn of an era; so I feel that there are many, many windows of opportunity. I think that online will be the place to be for exciting new techniques/technologies: video, audio interface, as already noted; convergence of qualitative and quantitative; mix of real-time chats and bulletin boards in one project; mix of chat and e-mail; mix of face-to-face and online, with the same participants; virtual ethnography (participants showing us their home) via digital camera. What an exciting place to be.

WALKOWSKI What parting thoughts would you like to leave with us regarding online qualitative research?

VAN NUYS Clearly, online qualitative research is here to stay. It will get better, incrementally, as we gain experience and share our own creativity with one another. And, unforeseen technological developments may catapult us into altogether new paradigms.

BÉLISLE I wanted to mention that one area we haven't discussed at all is analysis and reporting. Because online generates text transcripts automatically, it is now possible to automate some of the analytic tasks that are truly tedious when using tape-based data. I have used and can see greater development of macros and routines to mark text, search text for key words, convert text to citations, and so on. In a recent presentation I made about online research, the closing slide was of the Star baby from the *2001: A Space Odyssey* movie, and the caption was, (online qualitative will lead to) "a rebirth of qualitative research." Thus sprach Zarathustra!

ZINCHIAK At a recent meeting I was approached by another moderator who took great offense to the use of the term "online focus groups." We did not complete our conversation that day and she felt it was worthy of a Sunday phone call to me for debate. I have had other researchers try to pick apart the methodology, but never anyone take offense to the descriptive title. Seemed odd to me. Cyber groups, online qualitative, e-groups. Do you think our colleagues are receiving an injustice by using such a closely related term ("online focus groups")? Seems so minor, but she was passionate! Anyone else have this same experience?

VAN NUYS I know that chat groups have been criticized as not being real "focus groups" because there is a loss of group dynamics. I think there is some truth to the notion that the group dynamics are attenuated. This doesn't mean that chat groups are not useful, but it does underscore one of the ways in which they are somewhat different than face-to-face groups.

BÉLISLE The intensity of the response suggests that there was more at work than nomenclature. But I do agree with the opinion that "focus group" means something that cannot be further qualified, whether by "online" or "telephone." I don't think chat groups should be called focus groups, just as I don't think that telephone focus groups should be called focus groups. A focus group is a specific technique, and our industry associations have been derelict in not putting out a glossary of terms. I prefer to use the term "online" or "virtual qualitative" for the generic term, and "chat group" and "message board" for the specific techniques. Having said all that, I doubt that my opinion is going to change much, and I've given up trying. Monica [Zinchiak]'s post does suggest, however, that there are still some of our colleagues out there with a very negative view of online work. I was one of them, actually, despite my interest in gizmos and technology. The status quo can be a very comfortable habit, I guess.

WINTER A couple of years ago I felt quite strongly about finding a different name for them; so I wouldn't have to put up with people saying, "But you can't see the body language." Now, being even older and feistier, I am likely to respond, "Uh, huh. Now tell me something I don't know." (Okay, so

I've only wanted to say that.) I don't think the focus group term is too much of a problem. I do think, however, that chat has a negative and amateurish connotation.

SWEET At an association conference someone raised this question and suggested we give them other names. I leaned over to a fellow member and said, "I can hear it now. I tell the clients, 'I do cyber groups or e-groups.' And they say, 'What are those?' And I say, 'Focus groups online.'" I have no problem calling them online focus groups, and, in fact, one of my e-mail addresses is [xx]@focusgroupsonline.net. Guess that tells you how little it bothers me.

HERBERT Casey [Sweet], I couldn't agree with you more but I'm glad that Monica [Zinchiak] raised the question. At my company we call them CyberQual groups, and exactly as Casey [Sweet] says, everyone asks what they are, and then we have to tell them they are online focus groups. I guess giving things a name has two functions: accurately describing something and helping people to understand what you're talking about.

3.8 Epilogue

The members of this panel have more experience with real-time chats than with message board discussions. This suggests that, at the time of the discussion, real-time chats were more popular than bulletin board discussion groups among research buyers. That was two years ago. Currently, based on anecdotal evidence from online moderators and virtual facility vendors, the pendulum appears to have swung in the other direction. There now seems to be more emphasis on bulletin boards than on real-time online chat groups. We are uncertain as to whether this movement from real-time chats to bulletin boards will continue.

There seems to be a clear understanding today that message boards are more labor intensive (for both the researcher/moderator and the participants). Message boards can comfortably accommodate more participants than real-time chats. For these reasons, bulletin board groups are more expensive (on a per-group basis) than real-time chats. There is no doubt about the potential for higher quality and greater depth of responses from bulletin board groups, but it is uncertain whether the market will continue to support this costlier method of qualitative research online.

While real-time virtual facilities are designed to replicate in-person or telephone focus groups, bulletin boards represent a very different approach to qualitative research data collection. Whereas most qualitative research (online or offline) features a one-time data collection mechanism, bulletin boards allow us to collect data over a longer period of time. Bulletin board facility vendors tend to price their services on a short term (say, three-day) or long term (say, seven-day) basis. Some research buyers have inquired about extending the data collection period on bulletin boards to a month, several months, or even a year. Their wish is to have a customized panel of respondents to tap into for qualitative feedback on a continuous or ad hoc basis over an extended period of time. While this concept is very exciting, the logistical and cost issues of panel development and maintenance can be daunting, and the current pricing structure of most bulletin board vendors does not provide an incentive to use bulletin boards for extended periods of time.

Over the past couple of years, there have been attempts to bring audio and video to the online qualitative research arena. The idea is to use microphones and cameras to enable the moderator and participants to see and hear each other on a real-time basis from remote locations. None of these attempts, from our perspective, have caught fire. Perhaps current broadband capabilities are still too slow to provide sufficiently fluid audio and video streaming.

Market researchers tend to be a conservative, risk-averse group, and it is their conservative nature which acts as yet another barrier to adoption of online qualitative research methods. Research budgets are limited, especially in today's weak economy. As such, there is often reticence on the part of researchers or their internal clients to gamble on new methods that may (or may not, they fear) be advantageous.

Furthermore, the need for information to be delivered faster than ever so that decisions can be made further limits researchers' willingness to try a new method like online qualitative; the fear is that if the new method fails, there will be no time to re-execute the study using traditional methods.

How can more of the research community be persuaded to try online qualitative? One approach is to make sure that researchers realize that they do not need to take sides or to choose between online versus offline methods. Researchers need to understand that online represents yet another tool in the researcher's toolbox. They also may need to be reminded that the beauty of qualitative research is its flexibility. Those who doubt the utility or validity of online methods should consider employing both online and traditional methods in projects. A mixed-method or mixed-mode design represents a low-risk trial of online methods and enables side-by-side comparisons of methods.

Proponents of online qualitative research purport that the best measure of the validity of online qualitative is the extent to which the same conclusions would be drawn from parallel sets of online and offline groups. To what extent has this degree of success been achieved?

Those opposed to real-time online chats contend that in such discussion groups respondents speak tersely (using "sound bites") without any depth. Others might argue that real-time participants are simply being more succinct in their short responses. Setting aside the quantity of responses (number of words used by a respondent) online versus offline, are there any substantive differences in the quality and depth of responses online versus offline?

Anecdotal and proprietary evidence exists that online qualitative is valid research in that it leads to the same conclusions as traditional methods, but there is a lack of published evidence about the comparability of online and traditional methods. Appendix A of this book reviews one study involving online, face-to-face, and telephone modalities.

Chapter 4

A Focused Conversation

In this chapter we share our ideas about online qualitative research in a focused conversation. We thank Hy Mariampolski for developing the conversation guide and Itracks for allowing us access to its Bulletin Board Focus Group (BBFG) facility. What follows is the edited transcript from an unmoderated, open-ended conversation between the two editors of this book. It was an asynchronous conversation that took place during the first week of July 2002.

4.1 Is Online Qualitative Really Qualitative?

MARIAMPOLSKI Is online qualitative really qualitative? How do you resolve qualitative researchers' aspirations to be holistic with online's limitation to the verbal aspects of communication? What is being left out by focusing only on dialogue? How can it be replaced? Qualitative tries to be experiential, to see things from the respondent's point of view. How can this be approximated online? It seems to me that the moderator's role is more of a questioner than a listener.

MILLER Is it qualitative? Yes, I'd say it is. Right now, I'm participating in qualitative research—a focused conversation. There is a stimulus—a question from the conversation guide. There is an opportunity to respond in an open-ended fashion. No one is telling me what to type. I can express my "whole being," so to speak, if I want to. So I suppose it is "holistic" in that regard. I am restricted to using words, or to be more precise, all of the things I can enter from my keyboard and computer. If I had software for sending pictures, perhaps I could present a collage for Jeff [Walkowski] to see. If I had videoconferencing capabilities on my computer system, I could send a picture of myself sitting in my T-shirt and shorts and entering these words from my son's computer at home. Unshaven, glasses half way down my nose, leaning back from the screen with a wireless keyboard on my lap—not the prettiest of pictures. But, then, I'm not so sure much would be gained by your seeing me. Words can tell the story, just as they are now.

Dialogue is good for understanding the person; so is monologue. As for the moderator being more of a questioner than a listener, that would depend upon the moderator and the online method being employed. In an online focus group, as in a face-to-face focus group, the moderator can be dominant, assertive, asking all the questions, dominating the discussion. Or the moderator can take the more appropriate role of facilitator, asking open-ended questions that are intended to get participants talking among themselves. In a focused conversation like this, the "moderator," Hy Mariampolski in this case, is forced to be a listener. The moderator writes questions for the conversation guide and lets the participants go at it. So, Jeff, let's go at it.

WALKOWSKI I agree with everything Tom [Miller] has said. I have several additional points I'd like to make, as well. First, both online and face-to-face moderators can choose to be merely questioners and not listeners. Regardless of the venue used (face-to-face, phone, or online), the responsible and skilled moderator will not simply toss out the questions verbatim from the guide, and in the sequence they appear in the guide. No. The skilled moderator will think carefully about the relevance of the next question in the uploaded guide before sending it. He or she will carefully read all responses and probe for clarification or take advantage of opportunities to delve into discussion points not planned until later. So, if an online moderator wants to be more of a questioner than a listener, the capability is certainly there. However, the same can be accomplished in the face-to-face or phone worlds.

I disagree with the contention that online qualitative may be less holistic than other forms of qualitative. In the case of real-time online groups, it is much more than the mere text that the skilled online moderator should be paying attention to. The online moderator needs to pay attention to the swiftness of the reply (perhaps suggesting strength of opinion or attitude), length of responses (indicating whether they have a lot to say on the topic or not), and the use of punctuation and capitalization. It is my belief that online participants know that moderators cannot see their facial expressions or body language and that moderators cannot hear the inflection of their voices. They realize this and many will compensate for this by carefully choosing their words and by using the keyboard to convey this extra information to provide a more holistic impression of what they really think/feel/believe.

MILLER I think I understand the motivation for Hy's question—the online experience is different from the face-to-face experience. Perhaps being the online advocates that we are, we may be skirting the real issue. How is online different? And is it sufficiently different to raise questions about its legitimacy as a medium for qualitative research? Certainly, the physical experience of typing at a keyboard and reading from a monitor is different from the physical experience of face-to-face conversation, whether that be in a one-on-one interview or in a focus group. What is most obviously missing is eye contact. In normal conversations, we learn so much from the eyes.

WALKOWSKI What you say is true, but does that mean that a blind person cannot be a good moderator or qualitative researcher? I think blind people can be excellent moderators; they learn to rely on other cues to help them understand. Also, if qualitative research requires that the moderator listen (not just ask questions), there's no doubt in my mind that a good online moderator will listen, and demonstrate to participants, through thoughtful probes and follow-up questions, that he/she really is paying attention to what is being said and understanding fully what each participant is trying to say. What about this forum—this focused conversation where the questions have been "pre-programmed" with no moderator involvement included? It's more akin to observational research, which is a widely accepted form of qualitative research. No, the necessity to see the respondents is, in a sense, a crutch. I'm reminded of an article I read in a recent issue of *Quirk's* about this very issue (Yoffie 2002).

MILLER Qualitative research can be "observational," as in unobtrusive—set the stimulus, push the buttons, and let participants do their thing, all while staying safely in the background. That's a way to conduct research. Observe in the natural environment, including the natural online environment. The core of qualitative online is in the words, not the sounds or the sights.

WALKOWSKI I fear that we can easily slip into a digression on observational research and ethnography that has little to do with the suggestion that in online qualitative work, the reliance on words relegates the moderator to questioner, not listener. I think "the words" are key in all forms of qualitative group discussion (not observational research), but that other cues come into play as well. In the in-person arena, those other cues include body language, laughter, and other visual and audible cues. In the online arena, those cues include the particular choice of words, the speed of responses, and the use of punctuation and emoticons.

4.2 Social Implications

MARIAMPOLSKI If you acknowledge that verbal and keyboarding skills are differentiated among consumers, what steps can be taken to equalize the contributions of differentially able respondents? This differentiation seems to work against people who are already among society's outs—less educated, working class, poor, racial and cultural minorities, immigrants. How can you keep this research from reinforcing society's existing power differentials, from silencing the voices of people we need to hear from every once in a while?

MILLER I don't think that the online medium should be criticized for failing to cure society's ills. What can we do to provide access to the medium? We can collect data from Web-TV devices, kiosks, or computers in libraries and public access facilities. We can use research assistants to read or type for those who can't read or type. We can promote the use of videoconferencing over the Internet. Federal legislation relating to the Americans with Disabilities Act may spur the development of new Web-based technologies, providing wider access to the Internet. And we can take a multimethod approach, collecting online data from those who have access to and are comfortable with the medium, while using face-to-face methods for others. Does online have to be for everyone? I don't think so. If online methods don't fit the response needs of a target population, don't use them for that population.

WALKOWSKI When I teach prospective clients about online qualitative, so often they feel that they are being asked to take sides—to choose between one method or the other. It seems to be a revelation to many when I suggest that they may want to "mix up" the methods, if it will help them achieve their information goals. Online qualitative is an additional tool available to researchers. To echo your point, Tom, we need to pay close attention to who the target group is and use online qualitative only when it makes sense.

Another point: while online qualitative has the potential to exclude some social groups, it is important to keep in mind that it helps us to include others. For example, homebound, handicapped individuals and those living in rural locations are easy to include in online work.

Among those who do participate in online groups, there certainly are differences in terms of keyboarding speed as well as written communication skills. Just as in face-to-face and phone groups, it is the moderator's responsibility to see that all participants have a chance to contribute. Ground rules at the beginning of a group should state that typing speed does not matter, and that if a response to a question comes after the next question is posted, the information is valuable. Private messages can be sent to slow keyboarders acknowledging their contributions and encouraging their continued participation. Exercises can be devised to allow slower typists to have their say first, before others post their responses.

MILLER We seem to be in agreement that online research cannot be held responsible for "silencing the voices of people," not so long as we remain open to other research media. In terms of access to and coverage of a target population, we can make a strong case for multimethod research—research that makes use of more than one mode of communication with research participants. Not that multimethod research is a panacea—it isn't. After we collect data across a variety of media, we are faced with the challenge of combining those data in some meaningful way.

WALKOWSKI Absolutely. Mixing methods in a design might serve one purpose (using different venues to reach different segments of a target group), but it may create problems with analysis because different methods are used. But we're talking about qualitative research here. Even if a qualitative design calls for all online groups, or all in-person groups, many other variables can't be controlled; so comparability across groups comes into question there as well.

4.3 Process versus Results

MARIAMPOLSKI The entire book seems to focus on process rather than outcome. The purpose of qualitative research is not to produce nice, comfortable chats—it's to create better products, market things more effectively, give your client a foot up in a competitive marketplace. I'm not really hearing about how online can advance the client's, rather than the researcher's, interests. Is the insight produced by online different in any way from that produced by other approaches?

MILLER Process is important to getting to the outcome, whether the outcome be insights into a market, society, or the ways that people think. We are trying to learn about people by listening to the words they use. What we learn online could be different from what we learn through other media if (1) we are listening to different people or (2) people tell us different things online than they would tell us through other media. Sometimes we are talking with different people. Online research through the Internet gives us the opportunity to learn new things because it gives us wider access to the people who know things. Recall the panel discussion from Chapter 2. Lisa Kindig talked about getting medical specialists together for a focus group, and Bernie Klug described a global real-time focus group his firm had conducted.

Should we expect people to tell us different things online than they tell us through other media (face-to-face, telephone, mail, or facsimile)? Yes, people may say things online that they would never say in person or over the telephone. In a comparison of online and telephone responses we conducted for Mintel Ltd. (Miller and Panjikaran 2001), we found that what people said about themselves online was different from what they said over the telephone. One question, for example, asked people how many times they brushed their teeth each day. Online and by telephone most people said that they brushed their teeth twice a day. But online, a much higher proportion of people admitted to brushing their teeth only once a day. We might attribute this to the supposed anonymity that an online medium provides. In a telephone interview, the person being interviewed hears another person's voice in real time. Online, computer-mediated communication provides a different social experience. We should not be surprised when we learn new or different things online.

WALKOWSKI I think one of the reasons why we concentrate so much on process is because that is what so many researchers want to hear about. If they have not experienced online qualitative, the process is a mystery to them. Educating the research community about the process is a first step. I look upon online qualitative as being another tool for qualitative researchers to use. Some tools are appropriate for some jobs and not others. It's the same with online qualitative tools. Sometimes it is the best tool to use (e.g., for group discussion with a very low incidence group), sometimes it doesn't matter, and sometimes online is inappropriate (e.g., for taste tests).

My objective is to make respondents feel comfortable communicating with me, the researcher, and with other respondents. If the subject matter or the target group suggests that a study would be good to do online, I would think that, in the end, we will be providing higher quality information to our clients—information that will help them to make better (or at least, more informed) decisions.

MILLER Process versus insights? Yes, I suppose that we have been talking more about process, trying to educate the research community about online methods. Someday qualitative research online will be a common form of research, perhaps as common as face-to-face focus groups today. When that time comes, discussions of process will be passé, and we will see many examples of customer and social insights obtained through online research. How long will it be before that happens? Technology moves fast, and technology that reduces costs moves faster. Will online research advance the clients' interests? Of course it will. Clients love reduced costs.

4.4 Communication Styles

MARIAMPOLSKI I don't see anybody taking a critical approach to respondent utterances. Is there something qualitatively different about what people say in real life versus online? Do people shift their affect when they switch media? In my own work, I find that they do. (For example, in real life, I like to be very blunt and direct but I usually temper that with soft, slow speech and a big smile. Online, I find that it comes off as very arrogant and tactless; so I have to adjust my online persona or deal with the consequences.)

MILLER Researchers working in the domain of qualitative research will be better able to interpret online transcripts if they understand the nature of online communication itself. Computer-mediated communication is different from other types of communication. Online speech segments are shorter. The words may be blunt, more forceful, and more extreme.

In "Exploring the Possibilities of Online Focus Groups," an experiment with students at the University of Wisconsin–Madison reviewed in Appendix A of this book, we analyzed transcripts from online, telephone, and face-to-face focus groups. We observed shorter speech segments online, but curiously enough, we did not observe statistically significant differences in the proportion of speech segments that involved interaction among the students. Of course, many students today are comfortable with online communication. What makes online communication different from other forms? Typing, writing rather than speaking, time delays, the opportunity to correct what you write before you send it—all of these make a difference.

Social behavior online is an interesting topic. The bibliography of this book provides references for many books about behavior in "virtual reality," "cyberspace," and "cybersocieties" (Jones 1995; Porter 1997; Holeton 1998; Jones 1998; Smith and Kollock 1999; Rheingold 2000). On the subject of computer-mediated communication, I recommend Davis and Brewer (1997), Mann and Stewart (2000), and the edited volume by Sudweeks, McLaughlin, and Rafaeli (1998). Johnson (1997) and Lévy (2001) explore how technology and interfaces—Internet, desktops, windows, icons, hyperlinks, and agents—affect our lives. And Hale and Scanlon (1999) write about "wired style," noting the vagaries of English grammar in e-mail and chat.

WALKOWSKI My guess is that respondents' affect may be a bit different, but the crux of what they are telling us (the content of their messages) is the same. As a researcher who moderates online, I've discovered that I cannot verbalize online as I do in person. When speaking, I find I tend to ask a question and almost immediately rephrase it in the same "virtual" breath. I can't do that online, especially when I'm not using an uploaded guide and when I'm asking freestyle probes and follow-up questions. If I followed the same patterns online as I do in person, I'd spend too much time typing, potentially slowing down the group. In that sense, I've developed an online moderating style that is as crisp and succinct as possible. (I've come to realize the efficiency of that approach and try to be crisper and more succinct in my in-person moderating.)

My guess also (no formal studies on this) is that respondents are briefer in their online posts than they are in person. Most people are not natural born orators. In the course of a focus group discussion, they speak extemporaneously, and sometimes a participant may say a lot but take a long time to articulate clearly his or her thought. When I incorporate quotes from in-person groups in my reports, I am often taking a fraction of what a respondent says. However, when I include quotes from online focus groups in the report, I am likely to include a much higher proportion of the entire post. This suggests to me that because it takes longer to type than it does to speak, respondents want to use fewer words. In the real-time environment, they don't want to take too long to generate their posts. In message boards, they have the luxury of looking over their post and editing it as necessary before they send it on.

MILLER Computer-mediated communication is an area that offers rich opportunities for multidisciplinary research. Social scientists, marketing researchers, linguists, computer scientists (natural language processing and text processing experts), journalism and mass communication scholars—all can contribute to our understanding of online communication. This is also an area that will benefit from technological developments in text processing and text mining. Our discussion of online research has focused upon data collection processes—how we conduct online focus groups, in-depth interviews, or focused conversations. In the future, automation in text and data analysis will complement automation in text and data collection.

4.5 Online Transcripts

MARIAMPOLSKI Online produces instant transcripts alright, but are these more of a bother than they're worth? At what point does too much text become a problem for interpretation of its meaning?

WALKOWSKI I can't imagine that too much data is a bad thing, especially when it costs nothing to obtain. The trick is to know how to efficiently use the data. In real-time groups, the pace is often so fast and furious that it is difficult for me, as a moderator, to keep up with all of the details. In this case, the transcripts are a godsend. They help me to replay the discussion in my mind and get going with my analysis. Pulling verbatims from the transcripts in my reports is key to assuring that clients are simply not hearing what they want to hear and making snap decisions without considering all points of view heard in the online groups. In the message board world, the use of the method is often intentionally to get a deeper level of understanding from the participants. In that case, the need for transcripts is imperative.

MILLER I agree with Jeff, online transcripts are not a bother. These are the raw data of online research. For an asynchronous group, respondent postings may fall out of sequence, but, there is nothing to prevent the analyst from putting transcripts in correct sequence prior to analysis. Too much text a problem? Let's develop efficient algorithms for text analysis, natural language processing, and data reduction. In many situations, the words of transcripts can be converted into meaningful numbers for analysis. I am a big fan of words and numbers—can't have too many of them as long as I have my computer by my side.

WALKOWSKI I find transcripts from online groups easier to work with than transcripts from offline groups. With online transcripts, we always see the name of the person "speaking." That makes it very easy to spot topic changes (when the moderator speaks) and to track the thread of a conversation because we can see exactly who said what. Transcripts of offline groups do not break out who belongs to each paragraph.

MILLER Yes, in transcribing from tapes of face-to-face and telephone groups it is often difficult to identify who is speaking. We had this problem in our comparative study (Esipova, Miller, Zarnecki, Elzaurdia, and Ponnaiya 2000), as described in Appendix A. We were interested in studying interaction among participants; so it was important to identify each speaker by name. Many hours were spent listening to tapes to identify speakers accurately. Even with face-to-face groups, for which we had both video and audio tapes, identification of speakers was a hassle. Online transcripts were much easier to use.

4.6 Multimethod Research

MARIAMPOLSKI I don't think anyone is more in favor of multiple methodologies than I am, and, in my humble opinion, that's the strongest argument for online. How can online work with other methods? Which ones? (We've been trying to sell a combination of ethnography with online bulletin boards to clients. We see a very compelling rationale for it, but clients we've presented to have not been convinced.)

WALKOWSKI Often, the most appealing designs to clients are the clean and simple ones—those that do not mix methodologies. From that standpoint, I can understand your experience that clients have not been convinced of the value of ethnography with bulletin boards.

I'm going back to a point I made earlier. I had said that it seems to be a major revelation to clients when they come to me and ask me about the appropriateness of online versus offline groups in a particular situation. I always point out that they do not have to choose one versus the other, that, in fact, they are free to use both in a given project. This news is usually a pleasant surprise.

I've used the "mix 'n match" approach with clients who want to stretch their research budget further. They want to do as many groups as possible, and they know they should be going to multiple markets (or, at least two). What we've done is do in-person groups in their local market and online groups in more distant markets.

Here's another example of how different methods have been successfully used in a single study. The manufacturer of a high-priced sports car wanted to understand better the needs and perceptions of its existing customers. In-person, one-on-one interviews were conducted in one market where there was known to be a concentration of owners of this vehicle. A real-time online group was conducted with owners of the same vehicle in other parts of the country. In this case, recruiting for in-person one-on-ones would have been difficult in the outlying markets because incidence was so low.

MILLER Multimethod research—using more than one method or modality—may be misunderstood by clients. They may see it as an academic exercise: "research on research to learn about research." Clients get nervous; they worry about the costs and the time it takes to do multimethod research. To sell the idea of using more than one method, we need to show benefits, as Jeff does in his examples. Here are a few more examples. Multi-mode research with telephone screening and recruiting, followed by online data collection—this can be justified by the need to develop representative samples of participants who have opted-in to a study. Offering survey research participants the option of responding online, by mail, telephone, or facsimile, and offering focus group participants the option of face-to-face or online media—these can be justified by noting the need to provide access to a wide range of people. Conducting parallel studies with online and traditional methods—these can be justified when the client has concerns about the comparability of methods prior to a conversion from traditional to online. There are many places where multimethod research makes sense.

4.7 Is Text-Based Online a Temporary Method?

MARIAMPOLSKI Isn't online just a transitional and temporary method? If we had all the bandwidth we wanted, wouldn't we just go right to videoconferencing and run away from a purely text-based method? Or, is there something we would keep about a text-based approach that would be lost if it were all visual?

WALKOWSKI My guess is that Hy is right. If we had all the bandwidth required, we'd jump immediately to online videoconferencing. Most issues about missing body language would go away with this method. Why? Because it comes closest to the "gold standard" method of conducting qualitative research—in-person focus groups.

There are instances, however, when the absence of purely text-based online methods will be a loss for researchers and their clients. The anonymity that respondents feel in a text-only environment will be greatly lessened, and the extent to which they will be brutally honest with us may be lessened as well. As objective and as non-judgmental as I like to think I am, I am amazed to find out at the end of a group that a person is handicapped or is a certain age or whatever.

Who knows if my impressions of respondents, and my behavior toward them, would be different if I saw them in front of me (on the screen or in person). I would like to think that it wouldn't matter, but, as a fallible human being, I have to wonder how much I fall victim to that. So, I like the "forced blindness" imposed on all participants in a purely text-based online discussion group.

Getting back to the respondents, I have to wonder whether those discussing very sensitive topics (medical conditions, illegal behaviors) are better served in a text-only online environment. Respondents cannot see each other and, in that sense, are anonymous.

We would also lose the speed with which analyses can be done and reports prepared. In the videoconference scenario, transcripts would still need to be prepared. In the all-text–based scenario, transcripts are an instant by-product of the process. Certainly quick-turnaround transcription services are available, but they are expensive and not instantaneous. Thus, if we take away text-based online methods, we would lose some of the speed advantages (at the back end of a research project) of the approach.

MILLER Jeff gives good reasons for using text-only applications. Another is the act of writing or typing itself. Most of us are not always so coherent as we would like to be when speaking. We think and speak in "fits and starts." Writing and typing can be good—they slow us down. Editing and rewriting are also good. Recall the scene in the movie *A River Runs Through It* in which the father is home-schooling his son in the craft of writing. The boy brings his first draft to the father, who marks it up and tells the boy to cut it in half. The boy brings in his second draft to the father, and the father marks that up as well, telling the boy to cut it in half. Then on the third draft, one-fourth the length of the first, the father agrees that the writing is good. Some say that writing is thinking on paper. I suppose that typing into a response window is like thinking on a computer screen. I am a traditionalist. I like the fact that respondents are typing, especially when they take time to think and to edit while they are typing. Participant "self-editing" of transcript text helps the qualitative researcher, assuming that the essence of the message remains.

WALKOWSKI Your point is well taken, Tom. Still, we have to keep in mind that in some instances, we do NOT want respondents to think too much before communicating. This is especially the case in message board discussions, where respondents have the luxury of really thinking through and editing their responses; in terms of ad testing and probably most concept tests, over-intellectualizing about the ad or concept can lead us down the wrong path. This merely reminds us that online text-based tools are not ideal in all occasions, that they do not (and will not) serve as wholesale substitutes for in-person or telephone groups.

MILLER Yes, "intellectualizing" can be a problem. In some research contexts, we are interested in first impressions, and we want people to respond quickly to research stimuli, such as ads and concept boards. But I am not sure that text-only response modes are the problem. Rather, it is the fact that, with current online qualitative applications, participants must hit the "enter," "send," or "post" key before their text responses are transmitted to the researcher. It would be possible to develop applications that did not have this restriction, perhaps using data collection software that is downloaded to participant workstations. We could also impose time limits upon responses and/or tell respondents to respond quickly: "You have thirty seconds to tell us what you think of this product concept. Please respond with the first thing that comes to your mind." These are all things that we can do within the context of online research.

4.8 Final Thoughts

WALKOWSKI As more studies are published about comparisons of results between online and offline methods, I sense that qualitative research buyers will slowly come around and begin to use online. Especially in terms of online qualitative research, I've come to realize that qualitative research buyers are a conservative bunch. They are charged with selecting methods and vendors that will provide their organizations with information to help minimize the risks associated with making certain business decisions. If they have any qualms about the methods used to gather that information, they will shy away from it. They are often acting on behalf of internal clients and cannot risk collecting data in a new-fangled way that may steer the organization in an ill-fated direction. Their own credibility inside the organization, and perhaps their jobs, could be at risk with almost every piece of research they buy. For that reason, they will stick to the tried-and-true. Their biggest worry is that the results from online will be different from offline results. Published documentation about the similarity of offline and online results (or, the superiority of online results) will be essential to assuaging their fears. We are beginning to see these types of comparisons appear in the literature, and I think this will continue over the next several years.

I think many of us thought that online qualitative was going to be an easy sell. The obvious benefits of speed, geographic reach, anonymity, and the elimination of travel time and expenses were going to propel online to a larger share of the qualitative research pie than we see today. Personally, I was surprised by (but now understand) the conservative nature of qualitative research buyers. Thus, it is taking longer than expected. The bust of the telecom and high-tech industries and the rocky status of the global economy suggest that the penetration of Internet access from the home and the penetration of high-speed Internet access have slowed. This may have had an impact on the adoption of online worldwide (except for certain target markets, of course).

MILLER I am happy that Jeff has brought up the issue of client acceptance of qualitative research online. One of the reasons we are working on this book is to educate clients about the benefits of new media and, in that sense, promote more extensive use of online methods. Why have clients been slow to adopt qualitative research online? I think the answer lies more with costs than tradition. As long as the cost of running online groups is about the same as the cost of running face-to-face groups, clients will have little reason to switch. Lower the cost of running online groups, and clients will gladly move to qualitative research online. Automation is the key to reducing costs. At this point in time, Web-browser–based surveys are highly automated, employing well-defined sequences of questions, if-then instructions for branching, and computer verification of responses (checking for valid data types and ranges). Such automation has greatly reduced the cost of survey data collection. To lower costs for qualitative online research, we need to use intelligent applications that automate the process of data collection and analysis. Given the fast pace of technology, we have every reason to believe that such applications will be developed in the not-so-distant future.

WALKOWSKI In my practice, once travel expenses are considered, the cost of conducting online groups is less than offline groups. To your point, Tom, this is not enough for many clients. Not only are they expecting the travel costs to be eliminated, but they expect that the other costs of online qualitative research will be lower as well. I must admit that I expected the same thing when I first started dabbling in online. I thought that the recruitment process could be automated to reduce costs. I thought that incentives could be lower for online groups (since online participation requires less respondent time) and that facility costs would be substantially lower. Well, to my surprise, I discovered that non-personal (automated) recruitment ends up costing more in terms of disastrously low show rates, that paying lower incentives also leads to lower show rates. The lesson here is that we need to pay for the value of the information respondents provide—not for the time they give us. Online facilities can cost as much as (or more than) brick-and-mortar facilities. It surprises me sometimes that the travel expense savings is not enough to satisfy clients, but this is part of the adoption process that we have to address.

You say, "To lower costs for qualitative online research, we need to use intelligent applications that automate the process of data collection and analysis. Given the fast pace of technology, we have every reason to believe that such applications will be developed in the not-so-distant future." Whew! Those are bold statements! I'm not sure that I'm as optimistic as you are on this score. The very nature of qualitative research will make it difficult to automate the data collection or analysis process. True, there are tools available (and to be developed) to look for some patterns in the data. These tools can (and will) be used to jump-start analysis or supplement it, but they will never replace it. The artificial intelligence required to replace the current methods of qualitative data analysis and reporting are a long way off.

The approach taken with this focused conversation is an example of automated data collection. It probably works for us, but what about with regular consumers? Can we expect them to really stick to the topic, to provide us with the data we are looking for, without listening carefully to them and gently steering them to stay on the discussion path we would like them to be on? Perhaps, but I'm doubtful. Yes, the data would be qualitative in nature, but without interaction with the moderator and the insightful probes and follow-up questions he/she may ask, a focused conversation with a group of "regular" consumers becomes a glorified interactive open-ended question as may be found in a quantitative survey. Certainly that type of information has value, but it is less than can be gained by traditional qualitative methods with an involved moderator. Even in the current world, clients use open-ended questions, as may be found in quantitative surveys—that has value to them. They recognize that they would not be getting the same type of information if they were to allow the issues to be explored in a moderated group (whether online or offline).

MILLER Finally and thankfully, we have found an area where we can respectfully disagree. At the risk of being thought of as an eternal optimist with regard to technology, let me develop the automation argument a bit further. Though expert systems and artificial intelligence have failed to live up to the hopes of their initial proponents, there has been much recent progress in areas such as agent technology, computational linguistics, and statistical learning theory. Computer programs are not good at displaying common sense. Computer programs are not good at replacing real people (moderators or analysts) in ill-defined problem areas. But for many research tasks, even qualitative research tasks, we don't need programs that exhibit common sense. Many research tasks can be broken down into well-defined components amenable to automation or partial automation. I like to use the phrase "context-constrained automation." Computers are good at presenting stimuli. Computers are good at collecting and analyzing data. And computers are good at branching—doing A when X is true and B when X is false, where A, B, and X are well defined. What do we need to automate qualitative research? We need explicit, context-constrained research tasks, standard procedures, and conversation guides.

Not all modes of qualitative research can be automated. But new modes of qualitative research online will emerge in the near future, and the most successful of these (in the sense of being adopted by clients) will be those that reduce costs through automation or partial automation. The focused conversation in this chapter is an example of using an established online medium (the asynchronous focus group or bulletin board) to conduct a conversation between two "not-so-regular" consumers, to be sure. Notice the reduced cost—there is no moderator to pay. To what extent can this mode of online research be applied to "regular" consumers? That remains to be seen.

Chapter 5

New Directions in Online Research

Thomas W. Miller and Jeff Walkowski

> She touched the isolation knob, so that no one else could speak to her. Then she touched the lighting apparatus, and the little room was plunged into darkness.
>
> "Be quick!" She called, her irritation returning. "Be quick, Kuno; here I am in the dark wasting my time."
>
> But it was fully fifteen seconds before the round plate that she held in her hands began to glow. A faint blue light shot across it, darkening to purple, and presently she could see the image of her son, who lived on the other side of the earth, and he could see her.
>
> "Kuno, how slow you are."
>
> He smiled gravely.
>
> "I really believe you enjoy dawdling."
>
> "I have called you before, mother, but you were always busy or isolated. I have something particular to say."
>
> "What is it, dearest boy? Be quick. Why could you not send it by pneumatic post?"
>
> "Because I prefer saying such a thing. I want—"
>
> "Well?"
>
> "I want you to come and see me."
>
> Vashti watched his face in the blue plate.
>
> "But I can see you!" she exclaimed. "What more do you want?"
>
> "I want to see you not through the Machine," said Kuno. "I want to speak to you not through the wearisome Machine."
>
> "Oh, hush!" said his mother, vaguely shocked. "You mustn't say anything against the Machine."
>
> E. M. Forester, *The Machine Stops* (1909)

Minimal respondent burden, low travel costs, flexible schedules, wide availability with a Web browser and Internet connection, immediate, automatic transcripts—how can qualitative researchers ignore such obvious benefits? Moreover, how can we, as advocates for online research, explain the slow adoption rate of qualitative research online? Could it be their concerns about "the wearisome Machine"?

Drawing upon his early training as a biologist, the cognitive theorist Jean Piaget talked about two modes of learning: assimilation and accommodation. Assimilation is thinking about new things in old ways. We absorb or incorporate information, taking in novel stimuli and laying them upon already established cognitive structure. Assimilation is an important learning mode, to be sure, but one best suited to a stable environment.

Accommodation is learning through adaptation or modification of cognitive structure. We see things that don't fit our old ways of thinking; so we develop new ways of thinking. Accommodation is well suited to an environment in transition. It calls for change in cognitive structure to match change in the environment.

Online media and research applications are new. And, for many social scientists and marketing researchers, the languages of computing and data communications are new. To be understood fully, qualitative research online requires accommodation—academics and business people have to learn new ways of thinking about qualitative research.

Our motivation for working on this book has been to encourage others to experiment with online media and methods. As new methods of data collection and analysis emerge, it is our responsibility, being developers and users of methods, to ensure that the effect of technology is liberating and expansive rather than stifling or restrictive.

Tools for online research may be understood as general-purpose tools for collaboration. They have the potential of fostering productive communication across a wide range of application areas. Imagine teachers conducting virtual classrooms with the same software we use for online focus groups. Think of business meetings run with online focus group and focused conversation utilities. Clinicians can work with patients and investment counselors can advise clients using software for online interviewing.

What we learn from qualitative research online can contribute to qualitative research in general. Successful experiments with online focused conversation, for example, suggest new ways of doing offline research. Consider the possibilities—two participants in a room opening a series of envelopes with questions for discussion, self-moderating an offline focused conversation.

What do we mean by qualitative research? We start with observation, watching behavior in natural and social contexts, seeing communities at work or play, learning from what we see. Standing nearby the objects of our study, we strive to be unobtrusive, involved in observation but not directly involved with the objects of observation. Moving beyond observation, we interview, we listen, we interact. Our goal—to hear the voices of people in their own words—is consistent with the role of facilitator, encouraging discussion without influencing its direction.

If we were biologists studying ants, being unobtrusive and nondirective would be easy. But the objects of our studies are people. Research participants can see us and behave differently because they see us. Much qualitative research involves collaboration between researcher and participant. Interviewees know they're being interviewed. Focus group volunteers see the one-way mirrors. They expect to be observed, audiotaped and videotaped for research purposes. Accepting this truism of social research, we take the roles of participatory observers, interviewers, and moderators. We interact, we react to what we see and hear, and, like it or not, we influence what people do and say. It is a fine line between passive observation and active participation, between objective and subjective, between science and art. It is a line often crossed in qualitative research.

We have the participant and the researcher, and now we have the computer and the network. To say that the qualitative researcher's life won't change with technology is to ignore most of what happened in the latter half of the twentieth century. Technology will change the relationship between participant and researcher. It will have a continued and profound effect upon qualitative research.

There is a need for research on research. A number of issues merit study. Online qualitative proponents claim that respondents are more honest online than in traditional settings. Critics speculate that in the online environment respondents may actually take on different personas and be less honest than in face-to-face settings. We need to find out if there is evidence to back up either view.

Like the final scene of a play, a final chapter is supposed to "wrap it all up." But this is not the end of our story; it is more of a beginning. Qualitative research online is in its infancy. Exciting work awaits those willing to embrace technological innovation. The research world, along with the world of communication, is changing quickly.

Panels of experienced respondents have replaced samples of recruited respondents in many research settings. Building upon the success of self-motivated online communities and public chat rooms, some research providers have proposed the development of online communities of research respondents, groups of concerned consumers who are paid to discuss selected topics, such as their feelings about a brand or product category, over a long period of time.

Words of consumers and research subjects, user group discussions, logs from online chats and e-mail, real-time focus group and bulletin board transcripts—text from many sources is being stored electronically, available for future research and analysis. Researchers await developments in text analysis and text mining to help make sense out of these data.

Technology, the prime mover and shaker, shows no signs of slowing down. We are at the forefront of a new era in research. Call it "ultramodern" rather than postmodern. Rather than decrying the limitations of science, we see the emergence of a new technology-facilitated science with online methods permeating many forms of research, quantitative and qualitative.

Most of today's online research systems rely upon reading and typing of text. New systems are being introduced that combine text, streaming audio and video, and teleconferencing utilities. The Web as a transmission medium continues to expand through higher bandwidth and wider distribution. Computer system performance improves, and the development of agent-based technologies suggests further automation of research tasks.

Standards for information interchange like XML promote communication and collaboration among research entities, just as they facilitate interprocess communication among computers. We might think of the future research world as a collection of Web services linking networks of information providers and clients. The World Wide Web itself holds promise as an information store or "Semantic Web," a vast repository of machine-retrievable and machine-understandable data (Fenzel et al. 2003; Daconta, Obrst, and Smith 2003).

What shall we do about change? Adapt and accommodate. How shall we respond to new media? Use it in creative ways to enhance communication and research. Accept new technologies for what they can do. Be open to a variety of methods, both offline and online. Recognize that, despite the many ways we have of communicating and collaborating, we must continue to search for better ways of understanding one another.

Appendix A

Exploring the Possibilities of Online Focus Groups

Neli Esipova, Thomas W. Miller, Michal Zarnecki, Jason Elzaurdia, and Sanjay Ponnaiya

A.1 Introduction

What are the strengths and weaknesses of alternative modalities for conducting focus groups? How do online focus groups compare with other methods, such as telephone and face-to-face (in-person) focus groups? We answered these questions in a controlled experiment with a real-time focus group application.

The management objective of the study was to understand how students think about their academic majors and possible careers in business and marketing research. Administrators at the A. C. Nielsen Center for Marketing Research felt that this information would be useful in efforts to recruit students into the Center's graduate program. Subjects included junior and senior undergraduate students at the University of Wisconsin–Madison. Sampling frames were defined for three groups of non-business majors.

The experiment involved a balanced, between-subjects, completely-crossed factorial design with a standardized discussion guide. Subjects from each sampling frame were randomly assigned to one of three focus group modalities (online, telephone, or face-to-face) and to one of three focus group moderators. Moderators

---

Results from this study were initially presented at the AAPOR conference, Portland, Ore., May 2000 (Esipova et al. 2000). The authors thank the many people involved in conducting the study, as well as editing and reviewing data from the study, including Gala Amoroso, Karen Berendes, Laurie Borkon, Janet Christopher, Paul Christopher, Kristin Gill, Rebecca Kranz, Barbara Lindmann, Kelly Morales, Holly Pilch, and Krista Sorenson. Special thanks are due to Steve Cook and Siobhan Duffy for providing access to and technical support for FocusChat software (TNS Intersearch, Inc., formerly Greenfield Online), to Philip J. Stone and Vanja Buvač of Harvard University for providing access to and assistance with the General Inquirer program (developed with the support of Harvard University and The Gallup Organization), and to the A. C. Nielsen Center for Marketing Research and the University of Wisconsin–Madison for providing research facilities and support.

differed in the degree to which they encouraged interaction among focus group participants.

We examined recruitment success and completion times across modalities, moderators, and majors. We examined social interaction and reactions to a variety of questions. Response measures included counts of numbers of individuals volunteering to participate, numbers of volunteers actually attending and completing focus group discussions, and measures derived from the analysis of focus group transcripts. Results showed similarities and differences across modalities.

A.2 Methods

In this section we describe the methods used in the study, including the recruitment of subjects, experimental design, discussion guide, and transcript text and data analyses.

Recruitment of Subjects

Subjects for the study were undergraduate seniors at the University of Wisconsin–Madison. Lists of students were obtained from the university registrar. We defined three sampling frames for recruiting using lists of students from the humanities, social sciences, and natural sciences:

- Humanities. This sampling frame included students majoring in comparative literature, English, French, German, history, and Spanish.
- Social Sciences. This sampling frame included students majoring in anthropology, economics, geography, political science, psychology, and sociology.
- Natural Sciences. This sampling frame included students majoring in biology, chemical engineering, chemistry, computer sciences, electrical engineering, mechanical engineering, mathematics, and physics.

We recruited students by telephone using a standardized script. Students were offered $25 to participate in focus groups and were told that the discussion would take between one and a half to two hours. Randomized lists of student names and telephone numbers were constructed for each type of major. Prior to receiving the recruitment call, each student prospect was assigned to one of three research modalities: online, telephone, or face-to-face. That research modality (online, telephone, or face-to-face) was used in describing the research task.

To improve attendance at focus groups, one reminder call was made to each recruit either the night before or the day of the focus group. Our goal was to have exactly six participants in each focus group; so we recruited between ten and twelve students for each group. If more than six participants arrived to participate, we sent the extra participants into an overflow group. We used data from overflow groups to assess recruitment success only.

We conducted the focus groups from 4:30–6:00 and 6:30–8:00 P.M. on Monday, Tuesday, Wednesday, and Thursday. Each focus group began with six participants.

In one of the telephone groups, one participant dropped out shortly after the discussion began, leaving five members in that group. Actual beginning and ending times were recorded for focus group discussions; from these we computed the number of minutes to conduct the focus groups.

In recruitment for focus groups we did not control for the sex of participants. Twenty-six of the twenty-seven groups were of mixed sex; one group included only women participants. The topic for discussion, careers and attitudes about jobs in business, was an easy topic to discuss within mixed groups.

Experimental Design

The groups were conducted as follows across the three focus group modalities:

- Online. To conduct online groups, we used a real-time focus group application, FocusChat software provided by Greenfield Online (now part of TNS Intersearch, Inc.). Each online focus group was conducted by a moderator and a technical assistant at the University of Wisconsin–Madison. The moderator and technical assistant worked from a common workstation, with the moderator telling the technical assistant what to type. The technical assistant was familiar with the online software. The same person was used as the assistant for all online groups to ensure that moderator typing speed did not vary across groups. Participants in online groups had the option of working from any location having an Internet connection and a Web browser. They could work from their homes, dormitory rooms, or University of Wisconsin–Madison computer laboratories. Text transcripts with participants identified by first name were generated automatically from what student participants typed.
- Telephone. These focus groups were conducted through a commercial telephone conferencing facility. Moderators called into the service from a University of Wisconsin–Madison office. Participants called into the service from their homes and dormitory rooms. The telecommunications provider generated an audio tape and text transcript from each focus group. Because participants had separate telephone connections, the commercial provider had the ability to identify individual participants.
- Face-to-face. These focus groups were conducted at a focus group facility located on the University of Wisconsin–Madison campus. Face-to-face groups were conducted with a moderator sitting in a focus group room with the student participants. A one-way mirror separated the group from observers and videotaping equipment. In addition to their $25 monetary incentive, face-to-face participants were offered cookies and soft drinks. Audio tapes and videotapes were used to record the discussion. A typist worked from both audio tapes and videotapes to generate text transcripts with individual participants identified.

Moderators recorded clock starting and ending times for focus groups. From these we computed the number of minutes to complete the focus group.

Three women moderated the focus groups. Moderators were encouraged to act as they normally would act as moderators, keeping the same style across modalities and using words from a standardized discussion guide. To study the effect of moderator instructions upon participant interaction, three instruction types were used in the discussion guide:

- Moderator I. This moderator gave no instructions to participants regarding interaction.
- Moderator II. This moderator encouraged interaction only at the beginning of the focus group session. For example, the following words were included as part of her instructions for online groups: "Tonight's session is not intended to be a one-on-one discussion between you and me. This is a chat room, meaning that we all can talk together. My role is to facilitate a discussion between all of us as if we were interacting face to face. I would encourage you to communicate with one another and to respond to each other, as well as to respond to me."
- Moderator III. This moderator encouraged interaction several times within the focus group session. At the beginning of the focus group session, this moderator said: "I'll be moving us along from one topic to the next, but I encourage you to talk to each other, too, not just to me." During the session, she said: "I just want to invite you again to respond to what others are saying if you like, in addition to answering my questions."

The experimental design for the study may be described as a $3 \times 3 \times 3$ completely-crossed factorial design. Students were recruited at random from their respective sampling frames and assigned at random to focus group modalities and moderators. Major groups represented a blocking factor, crossed with modality (online, telephone, or face-to-face) and moderators.

When examining recruitment success, modality preferences, and questions about job preferences (which were directed to individual student participants), the unit of analysis was the individual participant. For other comparisons across research modalities, moderators, and majors, the unit of analysis was the focus group.

Discussion Guide

Using eight pretest groups, we developed a standardized discussion guide for use across each of the focus group modalities. Standardization was important because we wanted to compare results across modalities and moderators. There were differences across modalities in the initial and final instructions to participants and in the description of one of the projective tasks, a drawing exercise.

The discussion guide began with student introductions and a discussion of college majors and career goals. The guide included questions about salaries that participants expected to earn after graduation. Then participants were asked to make choices between ideal jobs and non-ideal jobs that paid 25 percent, 50

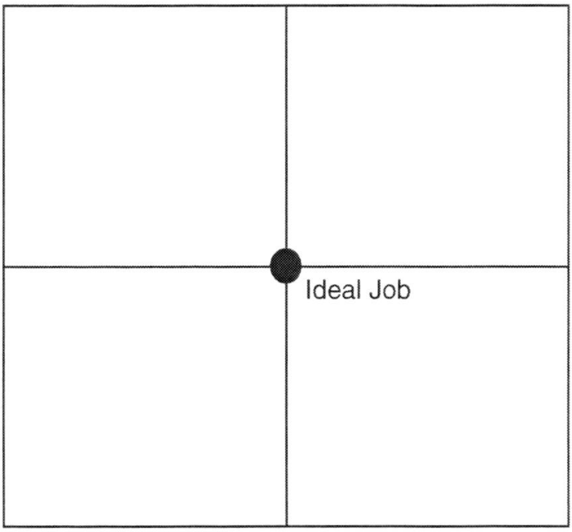

Figure A.1: Image for Drawing Exercise

percent, or 100 percent more. This was our attempt to observe potential differences in self report across the three modalities. Here is the text from the discussion guide:

> What would you expect to be paid in your first job after graduation? (Probe for annual salary if necessary. $20,000 a year, $30,000, $40,000, $50,000, $60,000? What kind of range would you expect?)
>
> Suppose you were offered two jobs after graduation. The first job is like your ideal job and pays what you expect to be paid in your first job after graduation. The second job is far from being like your ideal job but pays 25 percent more than the first job. Which job would you choose? (Clarify if there is a question about this. We are referring to jobs that the students could get right after receiving their bachelor's degrees.)
>
> Suppose the second job pays 50 percent more than the first job. Which job would you choose?
>
> Suppose the second job pays 100 percent more or twice as much as the first job. Which job would you choose?

Two projective tasks were included in the discussion guide. The first projective task was a drawing exercise that asked participants to plot points on a graph showing positions of alternative jobs relative to their ideal job. Figure A.1 shows the outline of the graph as seen by online and face-to-face groups.

For the drawing exercise, students in the online groups were shown a white board display of the outline of the graph and asked to make the outline of the graph on a blank piece of paper. Students in the telephone group were told how to make the outline of the graph on a blank piece of paper. And students in face-to-face groups were given a sheet of paper with the outline of the graph. After making their graphs, students were asked to describe them. Here is the discussion guide for the drawing exercise:

> Now we're going to use paper and pencil for a drawing exercise.
>
> [For face-to-face focus groups, hand out paper and pencils, hold up sample drawing, and use these instructions.] Look at this picture. You can see that your ideal job is in the middle. We will use this dot for your ideal job as a point of reference.
>
> [Telephone and online focus groups, use these instructions.] Draw a square box that fills about half the page. Divide the box into four sections by first drawing lines from the middle of the left-hand side of the box to the middle of the right-hand side of the box and from the middle of the top of the box to the middle of the bottom of the box. We'll call these middle lines "dividing lines."
>
> [For online focus groups, add this comment.] Click on this [URL image] to see the kind of drawing we are talking about, and then return to this window.
>
> [For telephone and online focus groups, complete the instructions.] Draw a large dot in the center of the box, where the two dividing lines cross. Label that dot "Ideal Job," to represent your ideal job. We will use this dot for your ideal job as a point of reference when placing other points in the box.
>
> Outside of the box you have drawn, write the following job titles: (1) Consultant, (2) Manager, (3) Marketing Researcher, (4) Salesperson, (5) Scientist, (6) Teacher, (7) Writer.
>
> Let's take a minute to think about these jobs and how they relate to your ideal job. [Pause for one minute.]
>
> Now I want you to make your box into a "job box." I want you to make a drawing that shows how the seven jobs relate to one another and to your ideal job. Draw a dot inside the box to represent each of the seven job titles. Draw the dots in positions so that the closer two dots are to one another, the more similar the jobs are to one another, and the closer a dot is to the center dot, the closer that job is to your ideal job. Use the job titles to label the dots. I'm going to give you about three minutes to place these seven dots on the drawing. [Wait for three minutes.]
>
> Now I'd like each of you to tell me about your drawing. What does the drawing say about you? What does the drawing say about the jobs?

> [Specific probes: Which jobs are closest to each other? Where does consultant lie in relation to your ideal job and to the other jobs? Where does marketing researcher lie in relation to your ideal job and to the other jobs?]
>
> [Other useful probe: Any other thoughts?]

A second projective task asked students to describe characters in a movie. The characters were consultant, manager, marketing researcher, salesperson, scientist, teacher, and writer. For example, the discussion guide for the scientist character read as follows:

> Suppose you were making a movie. One of the characters in the movie is a scientist. What kind of personality would you like the character to have? How would the scientist look? What would the scientist wear? What kind of car would the scientist drive? Give me a picture of the kind of person this would be.

Questionnaire

Following the focus group discussion, students were given a questionnaire to complete. Face-to-face group members filled out the questionnaire immediately after the focus group session and received their $25 checks the night of the session. Telephone and online group members went to an assigned campus location to fill out the questionnaire on the next or subsequent days and to receive their $25 checks for participation. There was a 100 percent response rate with all student participants filling out questionnaires. In addition to items relating to demographics, the questionnaire asked students about their willingness to participate in a future focus group study. In particular, student participants were asked:

> If you were given the opportunity to participate in another focus group, which of the following methods would you prefer? (Please check only one)
>
> ☐ Face-to-face focus group
> ☐ Telephone focus group
> ☐ On-line focus group

Text and Data Analysis

Three graduate students in marketing research were assigned to read and code participant interaction. A balanced lattice design was used to ensure that transcripts from equal numbers of major types, moderators, and modalities were coded by each graduate student.

To make comparisons across research modalities, moderators, and majors, we used summary statistics, trellis graphics, and classical hypothesis testing. We employed linear and generalized linear models, including Poisson regression for counts. Analyses were conducted using programs written in Insightful Corporation's S-PLUS, as described by Venables and Ripley (2002). Permutation tests utilized procedures developed by Hesterberg, as described in Hesterberg et al. (2003).

The analysis of transcripts began by arranging text into speech segments. A speech segment represented a collection of words or sentences by a single speaker. Speaker changes defined boundaries between segments. Speakers and receivers were identified for each speech segment. Word counts were obtained by using the word count utility of Microsoft Word 97.

The movie-making projective task was chosen for examining participant interaction. The movie-making projective task fell midway through the discussion, giving participants sufficient time to acquaint themselves with the focus group environment and with other participants and avoiding possible time pressure that can occur toward the end of a focus group. Transcripts were coded and analyzed for participant interaction using all participant speech segments within the movie-making projective task. Any conversation between participants not in direct response to a moderator question was coded as an interaction. Aggregating across respondents within focus groups, we examined the proportion of speech segments that showed evidence of participant-to-participant interaction.

Semantic content analysis of full transcripts was accomplished using the General Inquirer program (Stone et al. 1966; Kelly and Stone 1975; Stone 1997; Buvač and Stone 2001). We examined results across six semantic categories, representing three bipolar dimensions identified in Charles Osgood's semantic differential research (Osgood, Suci, and Tannenbaum 1957; Osgood 1962):

- Positive and negative word counts were based upon dictionary lists of 1,045 positive and 1,160 negative words,
- Strong and weak word counts were based upon lists of 1,902 strong and 755 weak words, and
- Active and passive word counts were based upon lists of 2,045 words indicating active orientation and 911 words indicating passive orientation.

Each transcript provided a word count on each of the six semantic categories. Word counts were divided by the total number of recognizable (tagged) words in the transcript to obtain a proportion of words associated with the semantic category. Recognizable (tagged) words were words included in the General Inquirer dictionary. Proportions were converted to percentages, and percentages were adjusted for differences across semantic categories due to numbers of tagged words in semantic lists. We obtained adjusted percentages assuming a base list of 1,000 tagged words. For example, the adjusted percentage of active words was computed by taking the percentage of active words and multiplying by the ratio (1000/2045), and the adjusted percentage of passive words was computed by taking the percentage of passive words and multiplying by the ratio (1000/911).

Table A.1: Recruiting Success by Modality

Index of Success	*Research Modality* Online	Telephone	Face-to-Face
Number of Calls	422	403	349
Number that agreed to participate (of those called)	116	89	92
Number that actually participated (of those agreeing to participate)	90	66	79
Proportion that agreed to participate (of those called)	0.27	0.22	0.26
Proportion that actually participated (of those agreeing to participate)	0.78	0.74	0.86

A.3 Results

Table A.1 shows recruitment success by modality. We see the numbers and proportions of students agreeing to participate of those called and the numbers and proportions of students actually participating of those agreeing to participate. Chi-square tests of independence showed no significant differences across modalities.

Table A.2 shows focus group means and standard deviations relating to the length of discussion, and Figure A.2 shows transcript length variations across the twenty-seven focus groups. Transcript length, as reflected by the average number of participant words, is shortest for online focus groups and longest for face-to-face groups. A Poisson regression model showed statistically significant modality differences ($p < .001$), controlling for differences across majors and moderators.

Table A.2 and Figure A.3 show that the number of participant speech segments was similar for online and face-to-face groups, while telephone groups employed considerably fewer speech segments. A Poisson regression model showed statistically significant modality differences ($p < .001$), controlling for differences across majors and moderators. The considerable variability across moderators provides evidence of moderator style differences; moderator II tended to cut off discussion sooner than the other moderators.

The length of participant speech segments may be computed by taking the ratio of the number of participant words divided by the number of speech segments. Table A.2 and Figure A.4 show that online segments were considerably shorter than telephone and face-to-face segments. This follows from the fact that participants in

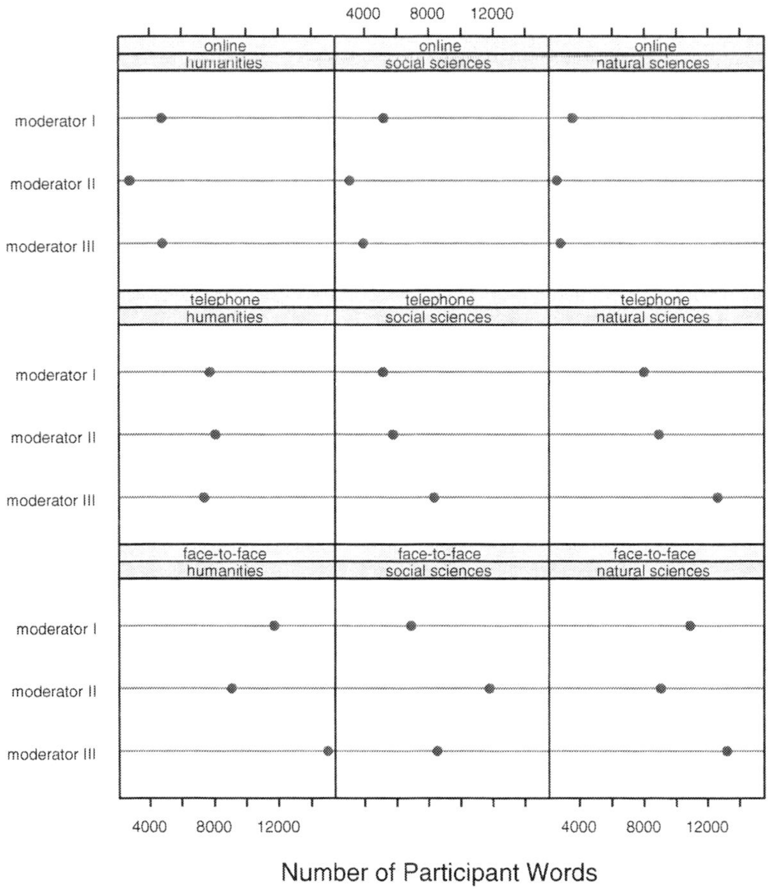

Figure A.2: Number of Participant Words in Focus Group Transcripts

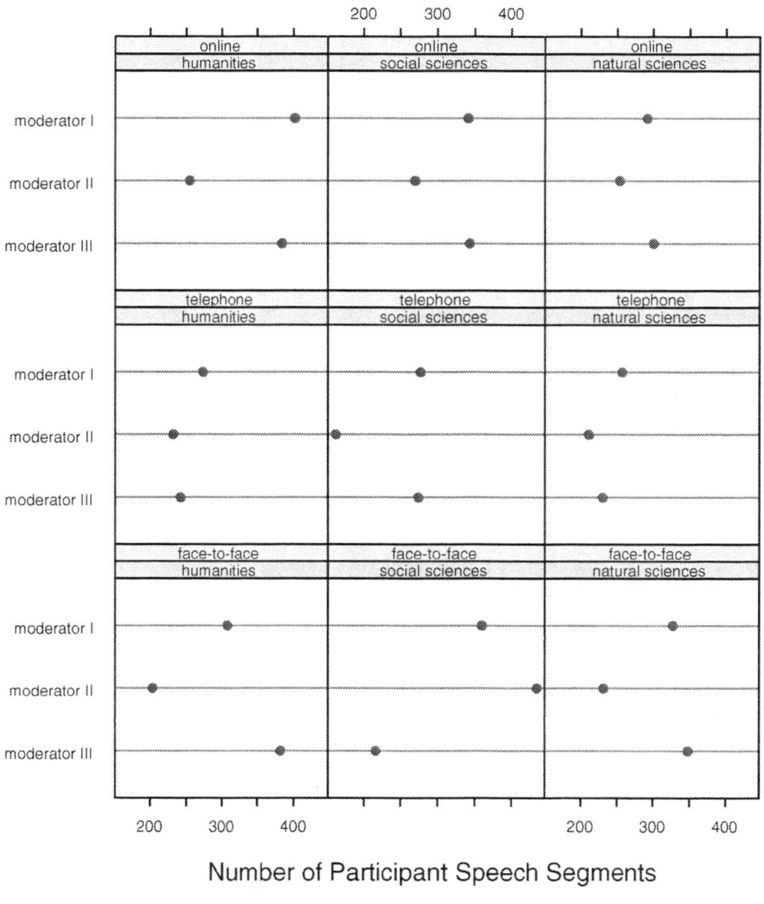

Figure A.3: Number of Participant Speech Segments in Focus Group Transcripts

Table A.2: Focus Group Summary Statistics by Modality

Focus Group Characteristic	*Online* $(n = 9)$ *Mean*	*SD*	*Telephone* $(n = 9)$ *Mean*	*SD*	*Face-to-Face* $(n = 9)$ *Mean*	*SD*
Transcript Length (number of participant words)	3,728	994	7,999	2,116	10,683	2,549
Number of Participant Speech Segments	316	55	240	37	313	80
Length of Participant Speech Segments (number of words)	11.69	1.65	34.06	10.06	35.30	7.75

online groups were typing and reading, rather than speaking and listening. A linear regression model revealed statistically significant modality differences ($p < .001$), controlling for differences across majors and moderators.

Focus group research modalities differ in the time it takes to complete discussion. Service interruptions, whether due to computer or network problems, made it difficult to measure discussion times for three of the nine online groups. Table A.3 shows the relevant data for the remaining six online groups, compared with the telephone and face-to-face groups. Face-to-face groups took longer to complete than telephone groups. Online focus groups took longer to complete than either telephone or face-to-face groups. A Poisson regression model revealed statistically significant modality differences ($p < .01$), controlling for differences across majors and moderators.

Further analysis of modality differences is provided by examining production efficiency across modalities. Using transcript length and the total time of discussion, we can compute an index of production efficiency, defined as the ratio of participant words to participant minutes. Table A.3 shows that production efficiency, like transcript length, is lowest for online groups and highest for face-to-face groups. A permutation test showed that the production efficiency of online groups was significantly lower ($p < .001$) than the production efficiency of the combined telephone and face-to-face groups.

Table A.4 shows participant responses to the question: "What would you expect to be paid in your first job after graduation?" Results are broken down by major group and modality. As we might expect given the types of jobs available to students, observed averages for natural sciences students are higher than for

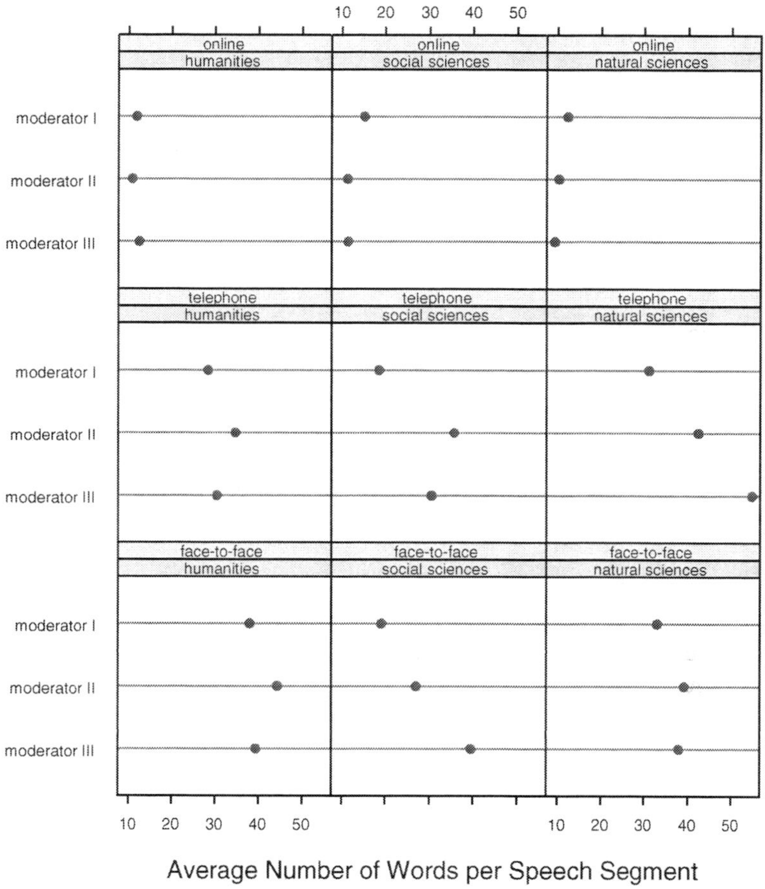

Figure A.4: Average Number of Words per Participant Speech Segment in Focus Group Transcripts

Table A.3: Time of Discussion and Production Efficiency by Modality

Focus Group Characteristic	*Online* ($n = 6^*$)		*Telephone* ($n = 9$)		*Face-to-Face* ($n = 9$)	
	Mean	*SD*	*Mean*	*SD*	*Mean*	*SD*
Transcript Length (number of participant words)	4,024	1,095	7,999	2,116	10,683	2,549
Time of Discussion (in minutes)	96.7	11.9	77.8	10.7	87.3	13.6
Production Efficiency (participant words per minute)	42.3	13.0	102.3	18.0	121.1	12.7

*Three online groups excluded due to measurement difficulties.

humanities and social sciences students. Observed responses were comparable across research modalities.

Following the expected salary question, we had asked students about their likelihood of choosing higher paying jobs rather than their ideal jobs. Table A.5 shows average proportions of students staying with their ideal job when the alternative job paid 25 percent, 50 percent, or 100 percent more. Observed responses were comparable across research modalities.

The drawing task provided evidence that tasks with complicated instructions and physical stimuli could be successfully executed within each of the three modalities. Students within online and telephone groups showed no special difficulties in making the drawings or in discussing the drawings afterward.

Social interaction was examined for the movie-making section of the discussion guide. Figure A.5, a trellis dot plot for the proportion of speech segments showing any participant-to-participant interaction, shows wide variability within moderators and within research modalities. Table A.6 shows means and standard deviations for the proportion of participant speech segments in the movie-making section that involved participant-to-participant interaction. We executed a set of six permutation tests for the proportion of speech segments showing any participant-to-participant interaction, comparing each research modality with the combination of the other two modalities and comparing each moderator with each combination of the other two moderators. No statistically significant differences were observed.

The follow-up questionnaire asked students to indicate their preferred research modality in a hypothetical future focus group study. Table A.7 shows that more

Table A.4: Average Expected Salary (Thousands of Dollars)

Major Group	*Research Modality*		
	Online	*Telephone*	*Face-to-Face*
Humanities	30.9	27.5	28.9
Social Sciences	28.5	29.7	27.3
Natural Sciences	46.0	39.2	45.2
Total across Majors	35.1	32.1	33.8

Table A.5: Proportion Staying with Ideal Job

Salary Increase of Second Job over Ideal Job	*Research Modality*		
	Online	*Telephone*	*Face-to-Face*
25 Percent	0.87	0.85	0.80
50 Percent	0.47	0.41	0.39
100 Percent	0.24	0.25	0.25

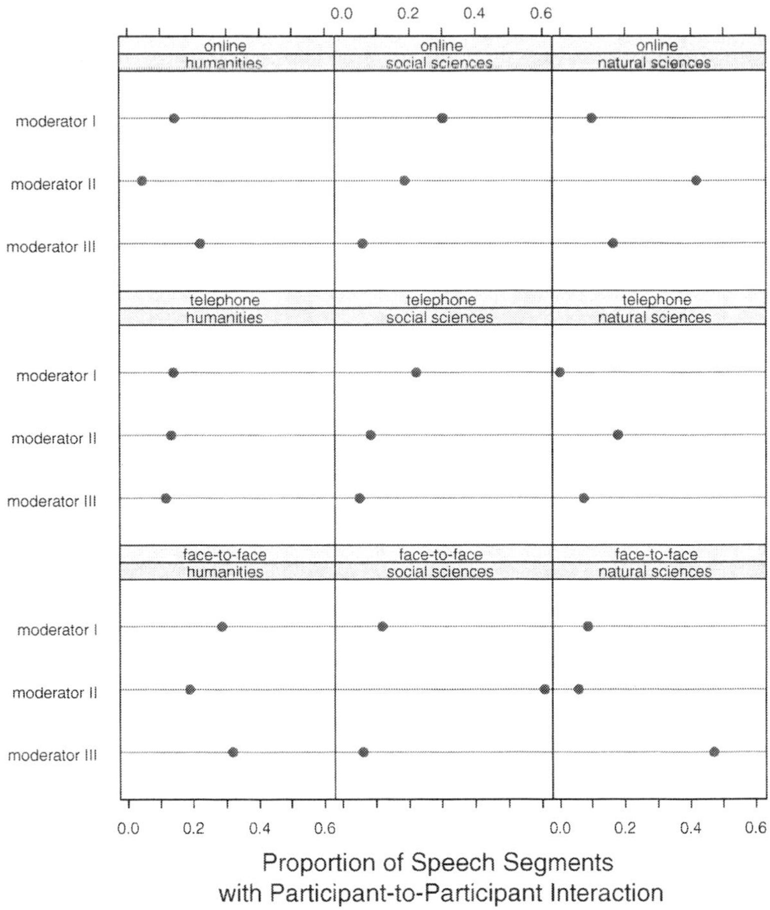

Figure A.5: Social Interaction within Focus Groups

Table A.6: Social Interaction across Moderators and Modalities

	*Proportion of Speech Segments Showing Participant-to-Participant Interaction**					
	Online		*Telephone*		*Face-to-Face*	
Moderator	*Mean*	*SD*	*Mean*	*SD*	*Mean*	*SD*
Moderator I (no special instruction to encourage interaction)	0.18	0.11	0.12	0.11	0.16	0.11
Moderator II (interaction encouraged only at the beginning)	0.22	0.19	0.13	0.05	0.29	0.29
Moderator III (interaction encouraged numerous times)	0.15	0.08	0.08	0.03	0.28	0.21
Average across Moderators	0.18	0.12	0.11	0.08	0.24	0.19

*Means and standard deviations computed across $n = 3$ focus groups for each moderator under each modality.

students indicated a preference for the modality that they experienced in this study than for either of the other two modalities. Many students in telephone groups expressed a willingness to switch to online or face-to-face modalities. Overall, face-to-face was the most preferred research modality, with half of the 156 students surveyed expressing a preference for that modality. Online was the next most preferred modality, while only 14 percent of the students surveyed expressed a preference for telephone. A chi-square test of independence revealed a statistically significant relationship between modality experienced and modality preference ($p < .001$).

Table A.8 shows semantic content analysis results, including means and standard deviations for the adjusted percentages of the six semantic categories we had chosen to investigate. The complete data for the focus groups are displayed in trellis dot plots provided in Figures A.6 through A.8. Permutation tests comparing the means of the online groups with the means of combined telephone and face-to-face groups showed that the online means were significantly higher ($p < .001$) for all semantic categories except the passive category.

Table A.7: Focus Group Modality Preference by Modality Experienced

Modality Experienced	*Number of Students Indicating Preference for Focus Group Modality*		
	Online	*Telephone*	*Face-to-Face*
Online	38	2	13
Telephone	12	19	18
Face-to-Face	6	1	47
Total	56	22	78
Proportion	0.36	0.14	0.50

Table A.8: Content Analysis of Full Transcripts

Semantic Category	*Adjusted Percentage of Words Coming from Each Semantic Category*					
	Online ($n = 9$)		*Telephone* ($n = 9$)		*Face-to-Face* ($n = 9$)	
	Mean	*SD*	*Mean*	*SD*	*Mean*	*SD*
Positive	5.59	0.42	5.00	0.37	4.89	0.42
Negative	1.14	0.14	0.67	0.11	0.77	0.18
Strong	3.88	0.56	3.26	0.18	3.14	0.21
Weak	1.60	0.26	1.18	0.18	1.17	0.14
Active	5.18	0.27	4.83	0.21	4.94	0.19
Passive	4.34	0.38	3.77	0.45	4.94	0.50

A.4 Discussion

Online offers a viable alternative to telephone and face-to-face modalities. This study showed that a wide variety of tasks and question types may be used successfully in online focus groups. Online recruitment and participation rates in this study were acceptable, and student participants indicated a preference for face-to-face and online modalities over the telephone modality.

Typing and reading take longer than speaking and listening. Using speech segment and transcript length statistics computed from simple word counts, the pattern of results is clear: real-time online focus groups take longer to conduct and yield shorter transcripts than telephone and face-to-face focus groups. A rough index of production efficiency (participant words per minute) computed in this study was highest for face-to-face groups, and higher for telephone than online groups.

The words people use when typing are different from the words people use when speaking. This study provided considerable evidence that the semantic content of online transcripts is distinct from the semantic content of telephone and face-to-face transcripts.

There were no statistically significant differences in the amount of social interaction within online, telephone, and face-to-face groups, as reflected by the proportion of speech segments showing participant-to-participant interaction. Neither was the amount of social interaction affected by moderator instructions encouraging interaction.

We urge caution in generalizing from the results of this study. The study used small groups of university students discussing their majors, careers, and job characteristics. Online groups were conducted with real-time, text-based focus group software and dial-up Web technologies available in 2000. With current technologies, we would expect to see fewer problems with computers and networks. Furthermore, the increased transmission speeds associated with broadband and DSL connections should improve the production efficiency of online groups. We encourage others to conduct research with diverse populations and with current technologies, so that we may learn more about alternative research modalities. Online focus group methods, both real-time (synchronous) and bulletin board (asynchronous), warrant further study.

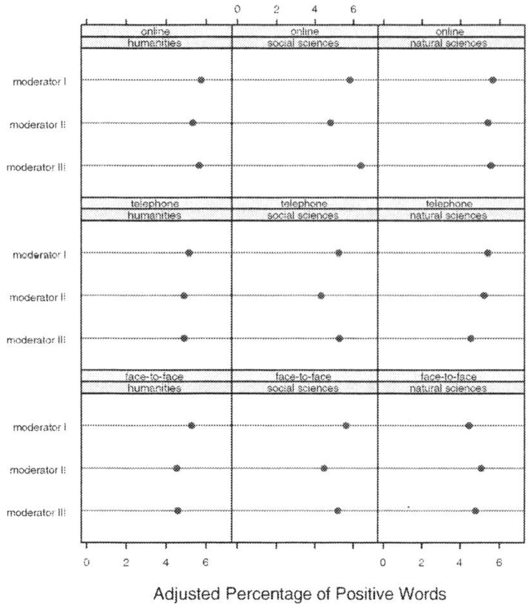

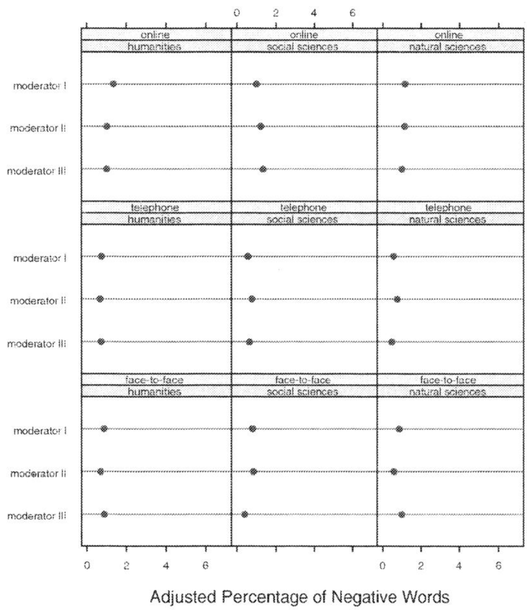

Figure A.6: Content Analysis of Full Transcripts: Positive and Negative Semantic Categories

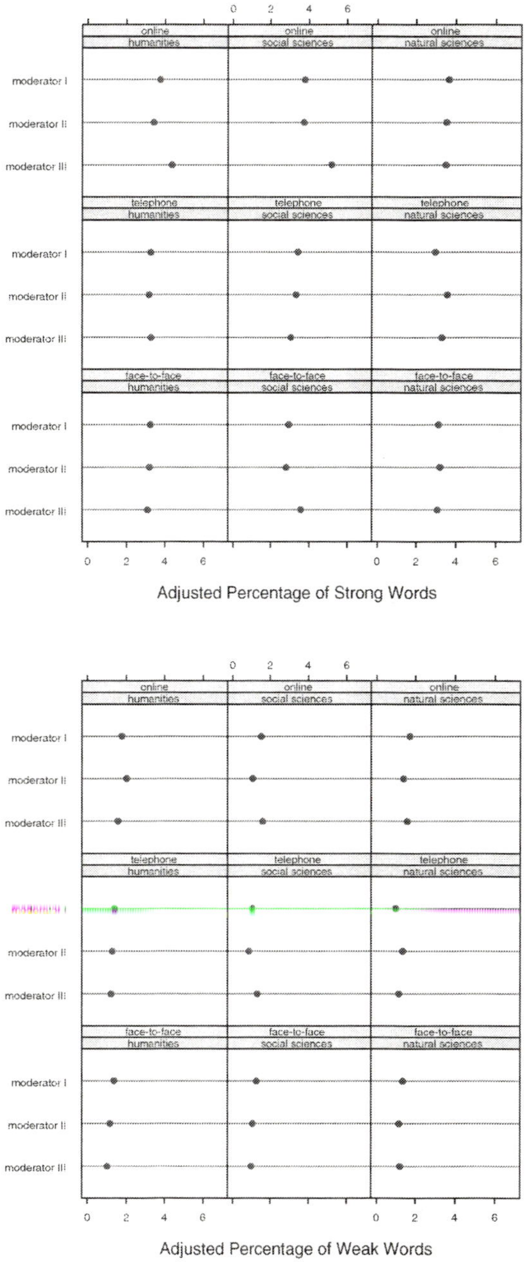

Figure A.7: Content Analysis of Full Transcripts: Strong and Weak Semantic Categories

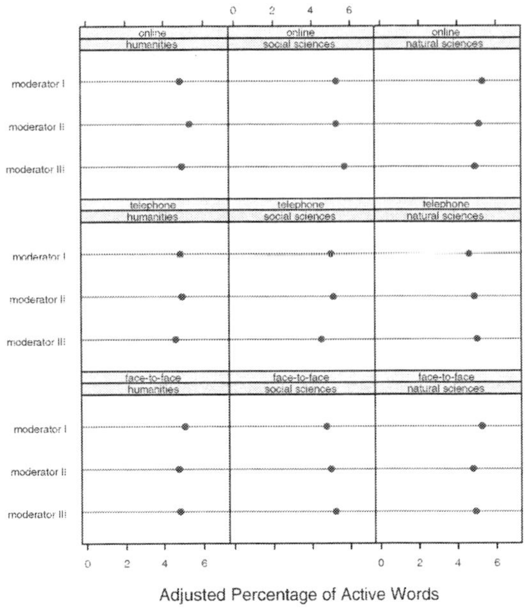

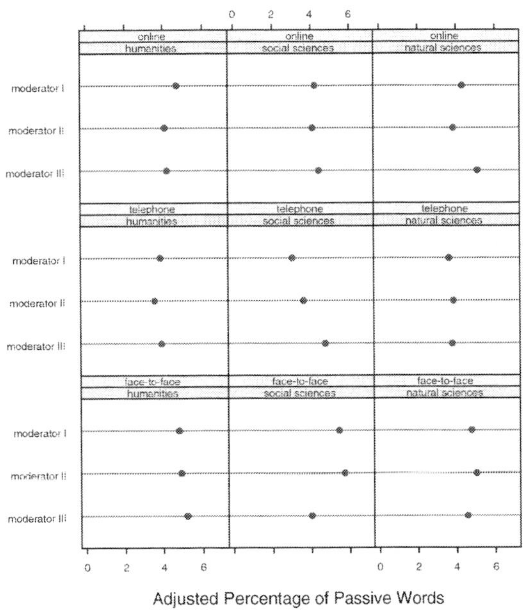

Figure A.8: Content Analysis of Full Transcripts: Active and Passive Semantic Categories

Appendix B

IMRO Code of Ethics

As a means of achieving and implementing ethical research practices, the IMRO endorses the following Code of Ethics:

The use of interactive and Internet research technologies provides an unprecedented communication mechanism for the exchange of ideas on a worldwide basis. These same tools also have the potential for misuse, particularly in consideration of the privacy rights of individuals. The Interactive Marketing Research Organization is founded on the principles of upholding the highest standards of both ethical and professional conduct in the use of research technologies.

Over and above normal standards of research, our professional activities shall be conducted with particular respect for the individual's right to privacy, both in terms of confidentiality of information collected during the marketing research process and the right to be free from unsolicited and unwanted contact.

Rights of Confidentiality

By default and design, confidentiality shall be granted for all information collected from customers and individuals and will be used for the clearly stated and intended purposes only. All personal data will be secured against access by third parties and/or unauthorized individuals or organizations.

Rights of Privacy

The right of the individual to be free from unsolicited contact is duly recognized. By default and design, customers and individuals will have the right to opt out of the research process. Specifically, IMRO members will abstain from the following types of surreptitious sampling and unsolicited or unethical recruitment techniques, known collectively as "spamming:"

Source: Interactive Marketing Research Organization (2003). Reprinted with permission of the Interactive Marketing Research Organization.

Surreptitious Sampling

Surreptitious Sampling can include but is not limited to the following:

- Collection of respondent e-mails from Web sites, portals, Usenet or other bulletin board postings without specifically notifying individuals that they are being "recruited" for research purposes;
- The use of Spambots, Spiders, Sniffers or other "agents" that collect personal information without the respondents' explicit awareness;
- The purchase of bulk e-mail addresses from sources that have not provided verifiable documentation that the individuals on the list have opted for contact for the purposes of research; and/or
- The use of client customer lists that have been assembled without the express consent of the individual for future contact via e-mail.

Unsolicited/Unethical Recruitment (Spamming)

Unsolicited/Unethical Recruitment (Spamming) can include but is not limited to the following:

- Unsolicited e-mail recruitment of potential respondents;
- Misleading or off-topic newsgroup postings designed to "trick" a potential respondent into participating in research;
- Junk mail sent in bulk to recruit for studies or panels;
- Scamming, which refers to the practice of recruiting under false pretenses (e.g. recruitment for research that is in reality a sales or contribution solicitation pitch);
- Spoofing, which refers to the practice of putting in a false or missing return e-mail address; and/or
- Chain or "buddy" letters aimed at recruiting respondents' friends, relatives or colleagues for studies or panels.

Responsibilities of IMRO Members

In all cases, the purpose of research conducted by IMRO members will be clearly and accurately stated along with the limitations of the use of personal information gathered. Individuals will have the right to be removed from potential research respondent lists and given a clear and simple way of communicating such a decision. Members will not willingly and knowingly mislead respondents as to the parameters of the research process including length of survey, incentive, use of data, etc. IMRO members will at all times conform to the 1998 Children's Online Privacy Protection Act (COPPA) and not collect personal data from children under the age of thirteen without the express approval of their parents or guardians. IMRO members pledge to comply with the local, national and regional laws and regulations regarding the use of all modes of data collection including both interactive and traditional channels of communication in the countries where research is being performed.

Appendix C

Contributors

Pierre Bélisle specializes in communications research and new product research for the high-technology and telecom sectors. Fluently bilingual in French and English, he is an experienced moderator and analyst of qualitative research. He has conducted research throughout North America and Europe. Since forming his qualitative consultancy in 1984, Pierre has worked in virtually every market category using a variety of traditional and online techniques. Pierre holds degrees in psychology (BA, University of Ottawa) and marketing (MBA, University of Toronto). He is a graduate of the Executive Solutions moderator workshop and has undergone training in Neuro Linguistic Programming and in the Osborne-Parnes Creative Problem Solving method. An active member of the Professional Marketing Research Society, he served on the Executive Committee of the Ottawa chapter and as representative to the Qualitative Research Division. He is active in the Qualitative Research Consultants Association, having acted as its Web master and served on its Board.

Jason Elzaurdia is with Chicago Investment Analytics, a boutique research group owned by Charles Schwab & Co., Inc. that specializes in quantitative equity research driven by insights from behavioral psychology. Jason's role is between research and product development; he works to match the development of the firm's research offerings with the needs of the institutional investor. Jason holds an MBA from the University of Wisconsin–Madison, with specialized studies at the A. C. Nielsen Center for Marketing Research. He also has a Master of Arts in English Literature from Northwestern University and a Bachelor's degree in Political Science from the University of Wisconsin–Madison. As a graduate student at Wisconsin, Jason was involved with the online focus group research undertaken by the A. C. Nielsen Center for Marketing Research. Also as a graduate student, Jason conducted a compendium ethnography study of Harley Davidson riders, and he designed and executed a university-sponsored survey of Fortune 500 CEOs. Prior to his MBA studies at the University of Wisconsin–Madison, Jason worked in marketing and marketing research in the financial services industry, specifically in the retail payment-processing arena for ARCO, First Data Corp., a Sanwa Bank subsidiary, and JCB Credit Card. In addition, he worked as an independent consultant to Mobil in the marketing of the Mobil Fleet Card and Speedpass.

Neli Esipova is a Consultant with The Gallup Organization, Princeton. She holds master's degrees in chemical engineering (MS from Moscow University, Russia), Slavic literature (MA, University of Illinois at Urbana-Champaign), and marketing research consulting (MBA, University of Illinois at Urbana-Champaign). Before moving to The Gallup Organization, Neli worked as Marketing Research Group Manager at the Wisconsin Survey Research Laboratory (University of Wisconsin–Madison), where she conducted various survey research and marketing research projects. Neli's research has addressed methodological issues, such as monetary and non-monetary incentives in online and mixed-mode studies, refusal avoidance and refusal conversion in surveys, and explorations of online research methods. While at the University of Wisconsin–Madison, Neli was involved with online focus group research undertaken by the A. C. Nielsen Center for Marketing Research. At The Gallup Organization she has been closely involved with online survey, focus group, and bulletin board research, as well as customer and employee engagement research.

Michael Herbert is the CEO of Michael Herbert Associates, a specialist qualitative research agency established in 1990 in London. This agency introduced online qualitative research with CyberQual in 1994 and conducted its first online commercial research project for the *Daily Telegraph* in 1995. The agency has been conducting online groups for clients such as Barclaycard, AOL, and the Electronic Telegraph. Michael holds a BA (with honors) in psychology from Monash University, Melbourne, Australia. He originally came to London as a doctoral student at the London School of Economics and never left. He regularly speaks about online qualitative research and runs Web research courses, which he has done for the Account Planning Group, Market Research Society, Admap, and the Association of Qualitative Research.

Lisa Kindig, Managing Director, Hall & Partners Healthcare, has over a decade of research experience, specializing in the pharmaceutical and healthcare industries. Lisa holds degrees in psychology and social relations (BA, Harvard University), arts administration (MFA, University of Delaware), and business (MBA, Fonbonne College). She has also been trained in qualitative theory and practice at the RIVA Training Institute. With skills in both qualitative and quantitative research, and using both traditional and online methods, Lisa helps her clients assess the market potential for pipeline compounds, develop new products, position new brands and line extensions, establish brand strategies, identify and characterize market segmentation, develop and assess messaging, evaluate professional and consumer advertising, and clarify improvements in education, sales and communications materials. Prior to joining Hall & Partners Healthcare, she served as a Vice President for Strategic Marketing Corporation, and as Senior Project Director and Team

Leader for Harris Interactive. Lisa is an active member of the Qualitative Research Consultants Association.

Bernie Klug is Vice President of Interactive Operations, NFO WorldGroup. His organization provides project management, survey development, and technical support for market research projects using interactive methodologies. Bernie holds a degree in computer science and mathematics (BS, Iowa State University). Prior to joining NFO, Bernie was Vice President of Operations for the ACNielsen Company and was responsible for the production and delivery of syndicated and custom marketing research projects. Earlier he worked for Donnelley, managing its household database and fulfillment operations.

Ben Lovejoy, Director of TNS Interactive, is one of the pioneers of qualitative Internet research. His experience of developing online services predates the Internet, having worked on commercial online databases as early as 1983. He was one of the very first researchers to use a laptop, projector, and a live Internet link to research Web sites in focus groups, and he is one of the acknowledged innovators of net-based qualitative research through virtual groups, qualitative e-mail panels, and teleweb conferences. Ben is a frequent speaker on Internet research at seminars and conferences, including Research99, the ESOMAR (European Society for Opinion and Marketing Research) annual conference, BIG, and the ARF.

Hy Mariampolski, Managing Director of QualiData Research Inc. since 1981, has training in sociology, social psychology, and cultural anthropology and holds a Ph.D. from Purdue University. Hy has conducted numerous ethnographies over the last fifteen years, working for clients in information technology, healthcare/pharmaceuticals, financial and professional services, consumer products, automotive, publishing/media, and retailing. His firm, QualiData Research, specializes in innovative qualitative research approaches to new product development and marketing. A pioneer in the application of ethnographic methods for marketing research, Hy is the author of several articles on the subject and has lectured, leading training workshops on the "how-to's" of conducting ethnographies. Hy has published the book *Qualitative Market Research: A Comprehensive Guide* (Mariampolski 2001). Hy received the Market Research Association's 1990 Annual Literary Award for his article "Focus Groups on Sensitive Topics: How to Get Subjects to Open Up and Feel Good About Telling the Truth." He serves as a member of the Board of Advisors of the Master of Marketing Research Program at the University of Georgia and has taught courses in research methods, qualitative research and focus groups at Kansas State University, Yeshiva University, and Hunter College of CUNY. Hy is a founding member and past president of the Qualitative Research Consultants Association (QRCA) and currently serves on its Board of Directors.

Thomas W. Miller is a consultant, writer, and co-founder of two research firms, Research Publishers LLC, a publisher of industry studies and research methods books, and Data Arts LLC, which specializes in systems for online research and data and text mining. Previously, Tom was Director of the A. C. Nielsen Center for Marketing Research at the University of Wisconsin–Madison, where he managed the Center's research program and taught in the School of Business. His prior academic appointments were at the University of Oregon, Hamline University, and the University of Minnesota. Tom holds graduate degrees in psychology (PhD, psychometrics) and statistics (MS) from the University of Minnesota and in business (MBA) and economics (MS) from the University of Oregon. His undergraduate training was in philosophy and the liberal arts at Ursinus College in Collegeville, Pennsylvania. For ten years Tom worked in the computer industry (NCR Comten and Hewlett-Packard), where he held technical, sales, and marketing positions. An expert in applied statistics and modeling, Tom has designed and conducted numerous empirical and simulation studies comparing traditional and data-adaptive methods. He is Chair-elect of the Statistics in Marketing Section of the American Statistical Association. Tom was instrumental in establishing the EXPLOR Awards Program for the American Marketing Association, promoting "exemplary performance and leadership in online research." He served as chair and invited speaker at numerous conferences dealing with online research and published papers comparing online and traditional research methods. His paper "Can We Trust the Data of Online Research?" received the David K. Hardin Award as the best article in *Marketing Research* in 2001. Tom is co-author with Dana H. James of *Marketing Research and Information Services* and author of *Data and Text Mining: A Business Application Approach.*

Sanjay Ponnaiya is with Ipsos-Vantis, the forecasting, modeling, and consulting arm of the Ipsos Group. In his current role at Vantis' Eastern Region offices in New York, Sanjay specializes in new product forecasting and development and manages key accounts in the financial services, alcoholic beverages, consumer electronics, and healthcare industries. Sanjay has quantitative and qualitative marketing research experience in all phases of the marketing research process, including study design, execution, and analysis. Sanjay's experience includes a stint at TNS Mode, India, where he worked on a broad range of marketing research projects, including demand estimation, product optimization, and communication route selection work, primarily focused on South Asian markets. Sanjay holds a Master of Science degree from the A. C. Nielsen Center for Marketing Research at the University of Wisconsin–Madison. Sanjay also holds an MBA from the Bharathidasan Institute of Management, India and an undergraduate degree in Physics.

Susan Roth, Director, Online Qualitative Research, TNS Intersearch, Inc., has considerable experience in the conduct of online focus groups and bulletin boards. She is currently in charge of online qualitative research operations for the U. S. offices of TNS. Prior to TNS, she founded the Qualitative Research Department at Greenfield Online and was responsible for product and project management, client and software development, and new business initiatives. At PERT Survey Research she served as manager of field operations, leading a team responsible for national mall intercept projects. Susan held management positions at TAi New Jersey and TAi Chicago, with responsibilities for focus group operations, client services, training, and research design. Susan holds a bachelor's degree from Denison University and is currently in a master's program at Wesleyan University.

Pat Sabena of Sabena Qualitative Research Services, Westport, Connecticut, has been in practice as an independent qualitative research consultant since 1965. She holds degrees in marketing (BS) and psychology (MA). Pat has conducted more than six thousand focus group interviews and one thousand one-on-one interviews among consumers, physicians, educators, and business executives, and has been doing online focus groups since 1998. Pat was elected and served as the 1995-1998 President of the Qualitative Research Consultants Association (QRCA). She serves as QRCA International Membership Chair. Pat has taught numerous workshops on qualitative research ethics and techniques in the United States, Canada, United Kingdom, Greece, South Africa, Australia, New Zealand, Brazil, Argentina, and China.

Casey Sweet, President of Quesst Qualitative Research, has over twenty years of marketing experience in product development, sales and promotion, and qualitative research, working with a broad array of industries. She holds an MBA from Northeastern University, a certification in Neuro Linguistic Programming, and has been professionally trained in moderation at RIVA Training Institute. She conducts both online and in-person focus groups with consumers and businesses. Casey has immersed herself in the online venue in recent years to understand how qualitative research can be conducted effectively online and combined with in-person research. Casey writes, speaks, and trains others in online qualitative research and has partnered with Jeff Walkowski to create OMTS (Online Moderator Training Services), an online training program to help professional qualitative researchers design and conduct online research. Casey is the creator and Co-Chair of the Online Task Force established by the Qualitative Research Consultants Association.

David Van Nuys is President of e-FocusGroups (www.e-FocusGroups.com), a San Francisco market research firm. He is also Chair of the Psychology Department at Sonoma State University. David holds a doctorate in clinical psychology from the University of Michigan. He has twenty years of market research experience, and his firm's list of clients includes many Fortune 500 companies, as well as numerous dot-coms and start-ups. David is a member of the Qualitative Research Consultants Association (QRCA), SofTech, and the American Psychological Association (APA). He is currently serving a two-year term on QRCA's Online Task Force, and he has been elected to the Board of APA's Division 32 (Humanistic Psychology). David's extensive publishing has included academic research articles, popular magazine articles, a nationally syndicated column, industry trade pieces, and, most recently, a book profiling the notorious Zodiac serial killer.

Jeff Walkowski is President of QualCore.com, Inc., a firm that provides traditional and online qualitative research services in Minneapolis. QualCore.com's client list includes Amazon.com, Pharmacia & Upjohn, SmithKline Beecham, Motorola, IBM, and TFA/Leo Burnett. Jeff holds graduate degrees in educational research (MS, Southern Connecticut University) and business (MBA, Southern Methodist University). Jeff is an experienced research practitioner, having had more than twenty years of experience as a provider of quantitative and qualitative research services. Jeff began his research career in program evaluation with the New York State Office of Mental Hygiene. In 1998 he ended a twelve-year career with M/A/R/C Research as its Director of Qualitative Research Services, and he founded QualCore.com. Jeff is an experienced focus group moderator and is active in the Qualitative Research Consultants Association (QRCA). He co-chaired the QRCA Online Task Force and chaired its annual qualitative research conference in 2001, one of the leading conferences in the area of qualitative research. He serves as the President of QRCA during 2003–2004. Jeff has developed and taught courses in online qualitative research and online moderating. In partnership with Casey Sweet, Jeff created OMTS (Online Moderator Training Services), an online training program to help professional qualitative researchers design and conduct online research. A recognized expert in qualitative research online, Jeff has been interviewed on National Public Radio's "Marketplace," and quoted in *The New York Times*.

Dan Weber is President and CEO of Interactive Tracking Systems (Itracks). Prior to founding Itracks, he worked for a management consulting firm. Dan holds a bachelor of science degree from the University of Saskatchewan. Itracks conducts online quantitative and qualitative data collection for market research companies. The firm was established in 1996, and its rapid growth can be attributed to leading, patent-protected applications for online focus groups and bulletin boards and custom survey development. Itracks' clients include ACNielsen, IPSOS, and NFO. Itracks received an honorable mention in the 2000 EXPLOR Awards competition, recognizing the firm's exemplary performance and leadership in online research.

Foster Winter founded Sigma: Research Management Group in 1981 and currently serves as its Managing Director. Sigma is a full-service marketing research company that offers qualitative and quantitative research, using both traditional and online methods. With the establishment of Sigma: Online Research Group in 1998, he has led the development of the firm's Internet research capabilities, including a virtual focus group facility and a wide array of Web survey methodologies. Foster holds a bachelor's degree in speech with emphasis in radio and television (mass communications) from Wayne State University in Detroit. With over twenty years of moderating experience, he has worked with organizations in the automotive, telecommunications, computer, consumer packaged goods, retail, airline, travel, manufacturing, and advertising industries. Prior to Sigma, Foster held positions in sales and marketing with Dayton-Hudson/Marshall Field's, Procter & Gamble, and Hallmark. He was also Vice President and General Manager of WGTU Television in Traverse City, Michigan. In addition to moderating over one hundred focus groups a year and managing research projects around the globe, Foster regularly presents seminars and workshops about online research. He serves on the Online Task Force and the Web Development Committee of the Qualitative Research Consultants Association.

Michal Zarnecki is a Marketing Research Project Manager for Abbott Diagnostics, a division of Abbott Laboratories. He supports the division in all primary and secondary market research needs for new product development, segmentation, positioning, and other marketing initiatives. In the past year, Michal has been primarily responsible for supporting the strategically important Molecular/Genetic testing area of the diagnostics business. Recently, Michal developed and implemented, with an outside research and technology supplier, a proprietary online panel of laboratory professionals. Since its inception at the end of the summer of 2003, the panel has been used for several studies that yielded significant cost and time savings. Before joining Abbott, Michal completed an MBA at University of Wisconsin–Madison, where he worked with Tom Miller and students at the A. C. Nielsen Center for Marketing Research, conducting the online focus groups project and exploring other online research initiatives.

Monica Zinchiak is the owner and lead analyst with Z. Research Services. Monica began her professional consulting career in 1995 and has sixteen years of professional market research and agency experience. Monica conducted many interactive media research studies in 1995, and since 1996 she has focused her business on the area of online qualitative research. Monica has conducted online focus groups for clients such as Clorox, GlaxoSmithKline, Yahoo!, Netscape, Hewlett-Packard, Intel, Sony, AT&T, Knight Ridder New Media, and various startups. Monica holds a BS in market research and her graduate studies concentrated in the area of psychology and social behavior. Monica is an active member of the American Marketing Association and the Qualitative Research Consultants Association, holding a seat on the Online Qualitative Task Force (2000-2002). Monica regularly speaks and publishes on the topic of online qualitative research.

Appendix D

Glossary

To understand qualitative research online, it is helpful to know terms that relate to qualitative methods, social science and business research, computers, online software applications, networking, and the Internet. This glossary defines technical terms and abbreviations used in this book. Readers desiring more complete dictionaries of computer and Internet terms can refer to Hale and Scanlon (1999) and Downing, Covington, and Covington (2000). Amor (2002) provides a good introduction to networking and the Internet. To introduce the glossary of terms, we provide a brief overview of the World Wide Web.

The World Wide Web arose from the marriage of hypertext and networking technologies. Its network foundation, the Internet, grew out of earlier wide-area networks, such as ARPANET and Usenet, serving the defense establishment, universities, and technical research centers. ARPANET was initially established for defense purposes, but became a wide-area network for many university researchers as well. Usenet linked many computers together in a simple telephone dial-up mode, permitting e-mail and file transfers. Standards-based networking protocols made Internet communications possible. Lower-level protocols defined how data could be reliably transferred over communication links. Higher-level protocols were developed for communication applications, such as telnet for terminal-to-computer communication and ftp for file transfers.

The idea for the World Wide Web was presented in 1989, while ideas behind hypertext date back to the 1960s. Hypertext—text with links to other text—represented a technology for developing dynamic documents, with the user determining the path between sections of text within documents. The hypertext markup language (HTML) that we use today was designed as a text-only system. Developers added markup codes to ASCII text files to provide formatting for presenting text content on a computer monitor. Software developers have, of course, extended these systems to present graphics as well as text. On the World Wide Web the hypertext links include uniform resource locators (URLs), which can refer to remote files and Web pages on the network or to local files and Web pages on the user's computer. Extensible markup language (XML) holds promise as a standard for information interchange, providing a foundation for interprocess communication and Web services. Further information about the Web may be obtained from the World Wide Web Consortium at `www.w3.org`.

Online research, both qualitative and quantitative, builds upon World Wide Web technology. Many applications are Web-browser–based. Some applications start by using a Web browser for access and then switch to another application or applet (often built upon the Java programming language) for running the study. Hypertext transfer protocol (HTTP) is the dominant method for client-server communication over the Web. In addition to Java, scripting languages like Perl, PHP, and Python, working in conjunction with Web servers and database systems, serve up the dynamic Web pages of online research applications. These research applications include online focus groups, focused conversations, in-depth interviews, and online surveys, as discussed in this book.

AAPOR American Association for Public Opinion Research. A nonprofit professional association that provides conferences and publications relating to social and public opinion research.

agent Also called an "artificial agent." A program that automatically performs duties for a computer user or a program that behaves like a person within a limited domain of operation.

AMA American Marketing Association. A nonprofit professional association that offers conferences and publications relating to marketing research.

ARF Advertising Research Foundation. A nonprofit professional association in the fields of advertising, marketing, and media research.

ARPANET Military-sponsored wide-area network, precursor of the Internet.

ASP Abbreviation for an Application Services Provider, a firm that provides outsourced application services. Also, in Microsoft systems, Active Server Pages.

asynchronous focus group See bulletin board.

bandwidth An expression that relates to the speed at which information travels over a network. The words "low bandwidth" mean slower speed and "high bandwidth" mean faster speed.

blog Shortened form of "Weblog."

bps Bits per second. Measure of speed across a communications link. Sometimes referred to as the "baud rate."

browser launch Some virtual facilities permit the moderator to open up (launch) a new browser window.

bulletin board Also called a message board or asynchronous focus group. An online application and designated Web site where participants (moderator, respondents, and observers) read and post messages. Communication can take place over a period of days. As an asynchronous group, it does not require participants to be online at the same time. The discussion is organized along discussion threads.

CASRO Council of American Survey Research Organizations. Provides codes of standards and guidelines for conducting survey research.

chat room A virtual meeting room on the Internet where participants gather and speak to each other. May be public (open to anybody, space permitting) or private (requiring passwords to get in).

client A computer through which users interact with the network or Internet. Web clients communicate with Web servers. "Client" is also used to refer to the person or organization for which research is conducted, the user of research and information services.

client-server application A computer application implemented with client and server computers communicating over the Internet.

collage A projective technique sometimes used in qualitative research. Respondents are given a theme and asked to construct a collage of pictures, words, drawings, or other artifacts, that represents their response to the theme. The collage is then used as a tool to help the respondents verbalize their perceptions, opinions, beliefs, and attitudes about various topics, brands, and issues.

cookie Data stored on a research participant's workstation that may be used to identify the participant and to keep information about past research transactions.

content analysis The analysis of the meaning of text from qualitative research. Sometimes called thematic, semantic, and network text analysis, content analysis often starts with simple word counts. Also see text measures.

corpus A document collection (often a collection of transcripts) used in text analysis and text mining. The plural is "corpora."

discussion thread A thread of discussion or conversation. See thread.

DSL Digital Subscriber Line. A form of high-speed Internet access offered by phone companies and resellers.

dyad A two-person group. Also used to describe a focus group with one moderator and two participants.

ethnography Observation in the field, study of social and consumer behavior in real life settings.

e-mail Store-and-forward method for sending messages over the Internet. Sometimes used for interviewing and for surveys.

emoticons Use of characters on a keyboard to indicate emotions in online communication. Capital letters can be used for emphasis or to indicate a raised voice. Some of the more popular examples with special characters include :-) for a smile or happy/pleased response, ;-) for a wink or "just kidding," and :-(for an unhappy or disapproving response.

ESOMAR The World Association of Research Professionals. Formerly known as the European Society for Opinion and Marketing Research.

EXPLOR The name, which stands for "exemplary performance and leadership in online research," refers to an annual awards program offered by the American Marketing Association.

focused conversation An open-ended conversation among online research participants with the focus provided by a conversation guide. Because there is no interviewer or moderator guiding the conversation, the focused conversation is participant self-directed.

frame An element of Web design. Some Web pages are constructed using frames, blocks of a page that a user can navigate within while all other frames remain static. For example, some online facilities utilize frames, with one frame for the chat stream, one for the text entry area, and another for stimuli to be displayed.

ftp File transfer protocol, one of a number of networking standards used over the Internet.

generative grammar Linguistic term referring to the rules that we use to form meaningful utterances. A general term for morphology, syntax, and semantics.

grounded theory A methodology for analyzing and interpreting qualitative data. Theory is derived from the data. The analysis involves identifying categories and coding data by categories. Common themes and concepts emerge from observed relationships among categories.

HTML Hypertext markup language. Standard codes used to format Web pages.

HTTP Hypertext transfer protocol. The dominant method for client-server communication over the Web.

ICQ I Seek You, a form of chat room software.

IMHO Shorthand jargon developed by online communicators, meaning "in my humble opinion."

IMRO Interactive Marketing Research Organization. Provides codes of standards and guidelines for conducting online research.

Internet A public data communications network consisting of many interconnected networks worldwide.

intranet A data communications network internal to an organization.

IRC Internet Relay Chat, a form of chat room software.

ISP Internet Services Provider. An organization that provides connection services to the Internet. These organizations usually provide software applications that run over the Internet, such as browsers and search engines.

IT Abbreviation for "information technology."

Java A general-purpose programming language introduced into the public domain by Sun Microsystems, with updates and support from Sun Microsystems. Especially useful in the development of online applications.

JPEG Graphical bit-mapped file format for images.

kbps Kilobits per second. Measure of speed across a communications link.

LAMP A public-domain suite for the development of online applications, this refers to the Linux operating system, Apache Web server, MySQL database, and Perl, PHP, or Python programming languages.

listserv An automated e-mail group. E-mail addresses of all participants (respondents and moderator) are programmed into a listserv. Moderator initiates the thread of discussion. Any response to that message automatically goes to anybody on the listserv.

LOL Shorthand jargon developed by online communicators, meaning "laughing out loud" or "lots of laughs."

Luddite A person opposed to technological change. In nineteenth century England a worker named Ned Ludd was supposed to be one of a group of workers who destroyed labor-saving machinery in protest for losing their jobs.

MEG Moderated e-mail group. Another name for e-mail group or listserv group.

message board Another term for an asynchronous focus group.

modem Modulator demodulator. Communications equipment that encodes and decodes data for transmission over a communications network.

morphology A branch of linguistics. Rules for forming complex words. Also see generative grammar.

MRA Marketing Research Association. Nonprofit professional organization for marketing researchers.

natural language processing Using grammatical rules to mimic human communication and convert natural language into structured text for further analysis. Natural language refers to the words and the rules that we use to form meaningful utterances.

netiquette Social behavior appropriate for working on the Internet. For example, typing USING ALL CAPITAL LETTERS is considered poor netiquette, as it is considered to be the online equivalent of shouting.

network Interconnected objects—nodes and the links connecting them. A data communications network contains computer system nodes and data communication links. The links are electronic circuits, wired or wireless.

offline In terms of qualitative research, refers to any methodology that does not make use of the Internet, such as in-person focus groups or telephone focus groups.

online In terms of qualitative research, refers to any methodology that makes use of the Internet, such as real-time chats, bulletin boards (message boards), and listservs (MEGs).

online community An aggregation of individuals that emerges through communication over the Internet. That is, a group of individuals that interacts online over an extended period of time. Also called virtual community. When used for primary research, an online community may consist of a group of fifty to two hundred people that have been recruited to participate in research about related topics over a period of three to twelve months. The research may incorporate a variety of methods, including online surveys, real-time focus groups, and bulletin boards.

panel A group of respondents that has been recruited to participate in many studies over a period of time.

Perl "Practical Extraction and Report Language." Text processing and scripting language used extensively in Web applications.

PHP A scripting language alternative to Perl, used extensively in Web applications.

post (noun) Posting made by a participant (moderator, respondent, or observer) in a message board discussion. A statement or question made by a participant in a real-time online group. (verb) To send a message.

provider Person or organization providing research and information services on behalf of a client or user.

Python A scripting language alternative to Perl, used for Web applications.

QRCA Qualitative Research Consultants Association. A nonprofit professional association of qualitative researchers.

real-time focus group An online focus group with the moderator and participants present at the same time. Sometimes called a "real-time chat."

semantics A branch of linguistics. The study of meaning expressed through language. Also see generative grammar.

Semantic Web An idea for having Web-based data defined and linked in a way that can be used by computers as well as by people. This requires wide acceptance of information coding standards such as XML.

synchronous focus group See real-time focus group.

syntax A branch of linguistics. Rules for forming phrases and sentences. Also see generative grammar.

TCP/IP Transmission Control Protocol/Internet Protocol. Fundamental protocol for computer-to-computer communications over the Internet.

telnet Terminal-to-computer communication protocol used over the Internet.

text analysis General term for methods of analysis and interpretation of text, including content analysis, grounded theory construction, and text mining.

text measures Following Miller (in press), scores on attributes that describe text. Text measures can be used to assess personality, consumer preferences, and political opinions, just as survey instruments can. Text measures begin with unstructured text (documents, transcripts) as their input data, rather than forced-choice questionnaire responses.

text mining The automated or partially automated processing of text. It involves imposing structure upon text and extracting relevant information from text. Like data mining, it is often associated with the analysis of large databases or document collections (corpora).

thread A thread of discussion or conversation. The sequence of online messages relating to a particular topic. Questions and statements that lead to other questions and statements. A term more prevalent in asynchronous focus groups (bulletin boards or message boards) than in real-time focus groups.

transcript The text log of a discussion, such as developed in an online focus group or focused conversation.

triad A three-person group. Also used to describe a focus group with one moderator and three participants.

Usenet Wide-area network precursor of the Internet.

URL Uniform resource locator, address for Internet information resources.

virtual community Another term for online community. Aggregation of individuals that emerges through communication over the Internet

virtual facility Adjective used to describe online the analogue of a real, physical research facility. For example, an online focus group software provides a virtual facility, analogous to a real in-person focus group.

Web Refers to the World Wide Web, available over the Internet.

Web board Another term for an asynchronous focus group.

Weblog A Web site with online information in a dated log format. Useful for individuals and organizations wanting to post current information about themselves.

Web server Networked computer that serves as the host for Web applications, such as electronic mail, listservs, and online focus groups. Contrasted with a client or computer where users interact with the network.

Web services With Web services, processes on one computer interact with processes on a second computer, providing interprocess networked communications. XML standards are used for information interchange.

white board A frame (window of a virtual facility) reserved for displaying images (visual stimuli, concepts, Web pages). Virtual analogue of a white board used in a meeting room for writing with dry-erase markers.

Wiki An exercise in collective expression on the Web. Software that facilitates the process of generating a Web site that is publically editable. Wiki Web pages may be edited by anyone at any time, from any device with Web browser access.

WWW Abbreviation for the World Wide Web.

XML Extensible markup language. Similar in structure and appearance to HTML, XML has a distinct purpose. It is a way of marking up data that describes the nature of the data.

Bibliography

Aarseth, E. J. 1997. *Cybertext: Perspectives on Ergodic Literature*. Baltimore: Johns Hopkins University Press.

Amor, D. 2002. *The E-business (R)evolution: Living and Working in an Interconnected World* (second ed.). Upper Saddle River, N.J.: Prentice Hall.

Bakardjieva, M. and A. Feenberg 2001. Respecting the virtual subject, or how to navigate the private/public continuum. In C. Werry and M. Mowbray (eds.), *Online Communities: Commerce, Community Action, and the Virtual University*, Chapter 9, pp. 195–214. Upper Saddle River, N.J.: Prentice Hall.

Bolter, J. D. and R. Grusin 1999. *Remediation: Understanding New Media*. Cambridge: MIT Press.

Borrull, A. L. and C. Oppenheim 2004. Legal aspects of the Web. In B. Cronin (ed.), *Annual Review of Information Science and Technology*, Volume 38, Chapter 10, pp. 483–548. Medford, N.J.: Information Today.

Buvač, V. and P. J. Stone 2001, April 2. *The General Inquirer User's Guide*. Cambridge: Harvard University. April 2, 2001. Software developed with the support of Harvard University and The Gallup Organization.

Charmaz, K. 2002. Qualitative interviewing and grounded theory analysis. In J. F. Gubrium and J. A. Holstein (eds.), *Handbook of Interview Research: Context and Method*, Chapter 32, pp. 675–694. Thousand Oaks, Calif.: Sage.

Cherny, L. 1999. *Conversation and Community: Chat in a Virtual World*. Stanford, Calif.: CSLI Publications.

Daconta, M. C., L. J. Obrst, and K. T. Smith 2003. *The Semantic Web: A Guide to the Future of XML, Web Services, and Knowledge Management*. New York: Wiley.

Davis, B. H. and J. P. Brewer 1997. *Electronic Discourse: Linguistic Individuals in Virtual Space*. Albany, N.Y.: State University of New York Press.

Dey, I. 1999. *Grounding Grounded Theory: Guidelines for Qualitative Inquiry*. New York: Wiley.

Downing, D., M. Covington, and M. M. Covington 2000. *Dictionary of Computer and Internet Terms*. Hauppauge, N.Y.: Barron's Educational Series.

Edmunds, H. 1999. *The Focus Group Research Handbook*. Chicago: NTC Business Books.

Ellis, D., R. Oldridge, and A. Vasconcelos 2004. Community and virtual community. In B. Cronin (ed.), *Annual Review of Information Science and Technology*, Volume 38, Chapter 3, pp. 145–186. Medford, N.J.: Information Today.

Esipova, N., T. W. Miller, M. D. Zarnecki, J. Elzaurdia, and S. Ponnaiya 2000, May. Exploring the possibilities of online focus groups. Paper presented at the American Association for Public Opinion Research (AAPOR) conference, Portland, Ore.

Feldman, R. 2002. Text mining. In W. Klösgen and J. M. Żytkow (eds.), *Handbook of Data Mining and Knowledge Discovery*, Chapter 38, pp. 749–757. Oxford: Oxford University Press.

Fenzel, D., J. Hendler, H. Lieberman, and W. Wahlster (eds.) 2003. *Spinning the Semantic Web: Bringing the World Wide Web to its Full Potential*. Cambridge: MIT Press.

Fielding, N. G. and R. M. Lee 1998. *Computer Analysis and Qualitative Research*. London: Sage.

Fuller, I. J. 1983, February. Electronic mail for the interactive office. *Hewlett-Packard Journal* 34(2):20–29.

Gauntlett, D. (ed.) 2000. *web.studies*. London: Arnold.

Georgakopoulou, A. and D. Goutsos 1997. *Discourse Analysis: An Introduction*. Edinburgh, U.K.: Edinburgh University Press.

Glaser, B. G. and A. L. Strauss 1967. *The Discovery of Grounded Theory: Strategies for Qualitative Research*. Hawthorne, N.Y.: Aldine de Gruyter.

Hale, C. and J. Scanlon 1999. *Wired Style: Principles of English Usage in the Digital Age*. New York: Broadway Books.

Herman, A. and T. Swiss (eds.) 2000. *The World Wide Web and Contemporary Cultural Theory*. New York: Routledge.

Hesterberg, T., S. Monaghan, D. S. Moore, A. Clipson, and R. Epstein 2003. *Bootstrap Methods and Permutation Tests*. New York: W. H. Freeman and Company. Companion Chapter 18 to *The Practice of Business Statistics*.

Holeton, R. (ed.) 1998. *Composing Cyberspace: Identity, Community, and Knowledge in the Electronic Age*. Boston: McGraw-Hill.

Holtzman, S. R. 1994. *Digital Mantras: The Languages of Abstract and Virtual Worlds*. Cambridge: MIT Press.

Huberman, B. A. 2001. *The Laws of the Web: Patterns in the Ecology of Information*. Cambridge: MIT Press.

Interactive Marketing Research Organization 2003. IMRO Code of Ethics. Retrieved from the World Wide Web on October 31, 2003, at http://www.imro.org/code.htm.

Johnson, S. 1997. *Interface Culture*. New York: Basic Books.

Jones, S. G. (ed.) 1995. *CyberSociety: Computer-Mediated Communication and Community*. Thousand Oaks, Calif.: Sage.

Jones, S. G. (ed.) 1997. *Virtual Culture: Identity & Communication in Cybersociety*. Thousand Oaks, Calif.: Sage.

Jones, S. G. (ed.) 1998. *CyberSociety 2.0: Revisiting Computer-Mediated Communication and Community*. Thousand Oaks, Calif.: Sage.

Jones, S. G. (ed.) 1999. *Doing Internet Research: Critical Issues and Methods for Examining the Net*. Thousand Oaks, Calif.: Sage.

Jonscher, C. 1999. *The Evolution of Wired Life: From the Alphabet to the Soul-Catcher Chip—How Information Technologies Change Our World*. New York: Wiley.

Kelle, U. (ed.) 1995. *Computer-Aided Qualitative Data Analysis: Theory, Methods, and Practice*. London: Sage.

Kelly, E. F. and P. J. Stone (eds.) 1975. *Computer Recognition of English Word Senses*. Amsterdam: North-Holland.

Kohda, Y., H. Sugano, and S. Okuyama 2000, December. IMPP: A new instant messaging standard and its impact on Internet business. *FUJITSU Science and Technology Journal* 36(2):147–153.

Krueger, R. A. 1998. *Moderating Focus Groups*. Thousand Oaks, Calif.: Sage.

Kvale, S. 1996. *InterViews: An Introduction to Qualitative Research Interviewing*. Thousand Oaks, Calif.: Sage.

Langer, J. 2001. *The Mirrowed Window: Focus Groups from a Moderator's Point of View*. Ithaca, N.Y.: Paramount Market Publishing.

Lévy, P. 1997. *Collective Intelligence: Mankind's Emerging World in Cyberspace*. Cambridge, Mass.: Perseus Books.

Lévy, P. 2001. *Cyberculture*. Minneapolis: University of Minnesota Press.

Lindahl, C. and E. Blount 2003. Weblogs: Simplifying web publishing. *Computer* 36(11):114–116.

Lovejoy, B. 2000. Online qual: The good, the bad, & the ugly. ESOMAR Net Effects[3]. Retrieved from http://www.tnsofres.com/industryexpertise/internet/esomar.pdf.

Lunenfeld, P. 2000. *Snap to Grid: A User's Guide to Digital Arts, Media, and Cultures*. Cambridge: MIT Press.

Mann, C. and F. Stewart 2000. *Internet Communication and Qualitative Research: A Handbook for Researching Online*. London: Sage.

Mann, C. and F. Stewart 2002. Internet interviewing. In J. F. Gubrium and J. A. Holstein (eds.), *Handbook of Interview Research: Context and Method*, Chapter 29, pp. 603–627. Thousand Oaks, Calif.: Sage.

Mariampolski, H. 2001. *Qualitative Market Research: A Comprehensive Guide*. Thousand Oaks, Calif.: Sage.

Markham, A. N. 1998. *Life Online: Researching Real Experience in Virtual Space*. Walnut Creek, Calif.: AltaMira Press.

McArthur, R. and P. Bruza 2001. The ABCs of online community. In N. Zhong, Y. Yao, J. Liu, and S. Ohsuga (eds.), *Web Intelligence: Research and Development*, pp. 141–147. New York: Springer.

McLuhan, M. 1965. *Understanding Media*. New York: McGraw-Hill.

Miller, D. and D. Slater 2000. *The Internet: An Ethnographic Approach*. Oxford: Berg.

Miller, T. W. 2000. Marketing research and the information industry. *CASRO Journal 2000*:21–26.

Miller, T. W. 2001, Summer. Can we trust the data of online research? *Marketing Research*:26–32.

Miller, T. W. 2002. Propensity scoring for multimethod research. *Canadian Journal of Marketing Research* 20(2):46–61.

Miller, T. W. 2005. *Data and Text Mining: A Business Application Approach*. Upper Saddle River, N.J.: Prentice Hall.

Miller, T. W. and P. R. Dickson 2001. On-line market research. *International Journal of Electronic Commerce* 5(3):139–167.

Miller, T. W. and D. H. James 2003. *Marketing Research and Information Services: 2003 Industry Report*. Milton, Wis.: Research Publishers.

Miller, T. W. and K. J. Panjikaran 2001. Studies in comparability: The propensity scoring approach. Research Report, A. C. Nielsen Center for Marketing Research, University of Wisconsin–Madison, Madison, Wis.

Miller, T. W., D. Rake, T. Sumimoto, and P. S. Hollman 2001. Reliability and comparability of choice-based measures: Online and paper-and-pencil methods of administration. *2001 Sawtooth Software Conference Proceedings*:123–130. Published by Sawtooth Software, Sequim, Wash.

Neuendorf, K. A. 2002. *The Content Analysis Guidebook*. Thousand Oaks, Calif.: Sage.

Osgood, C. 1962. Studies in the generality of affective meaning systems. *American Psychologist* 17:10–28.

Osgood, C., G. Suci, and P. Tannenbaum (eds.) 1957. *The Measurement of Meaning*. Urbana, Ill.: University of Illinois Press.

Piaget, J. 1966. *Psychology of Intelligence*. Totowa, N.J.: Littlefield, Adams & Company. First published in France in 1947 as *La Psychologie de L'Intelligence*.

Popping, R. 2000. *Computer-Assisted Text Analysis*. Thousand Oaks, Calif.: Sage.

Porter, D. (ed.) 1997. *Internet Culture*. New York: Routledge.

Powazak, D. M. 2001. *Design for Community: The Art of Connecting Real People in Virtual Places*. Indianapolis: New Riders.

Preece, J. 2000. *Online Communities: Designing Usability, Supporting Sociability*. New York: Wiley.

Rheingold, H. 2000. *The Virtual Community: Homesteading on the Electronic Frontier* (revised ed.). Cambridge: The MIT Press.

Roberts, C. W. (ed.) 1997. *Text Analysis for the Social Sciences: Methods for Drawing Statistical Inferences from Texts and Transcripts*. Mahway, N.J.: Lawrence Erlbaum Associates.

Ryan, G. W. and H. R. Bernard 2000. Data management and analysis methods. In N. K. Denzin and Y. S. Lincoln (eds.), *Handbook of Qualitative Research: Context and Method* (second ed.), Chapter 29, pp. 769–802. Thousand Oaks, Calif.: Sage.

Ryan, M.-L. (ed.) 1999. *Cyberspace Textuality: Computer Technology and Literary Theory*. Bloomington, Ind.: Indiana University Press.

Salmon, G. 2000. *E-Moderating: The Key to Teaching and Learning Online*. London: Kogan Page.

Scholder, A. and J. Crandall (eds.) 2001. *Interaction: Artistic Practice in the Network*. New York: Distributed Art Publishers.

Schrott, P. R. and D. J. Lanoue 1994. Trends and perspectives in content analysis. In I. Borg and P. Mohler (eds.), *Trends and Perspectives in Empirical Social Research*, pp. 327–345. Berlin: Walter de Gruyter.

Seale, C. 2002. Computer-assisted analysis of qualitative interview data. In J. F. Gubrium and J. A. Holstein (eds.), *Handbook of Interview Research: Context and Method*, Chapter 31, pp. 651–670. Thousand Oaks, Calif.: Sage.

Sharf, B. F. 1999. Beyond netiquette: The ethics of doing naturalistic discourse research on the internet. In S. Jones (ed.), *Doing Internet Research: Critical Issues and Methods for Examining the Net*, Chapter 12, pp. 243–256. Thousand Oaks, Calif.: Sage.

Sherry, Jr., J. F. and R. V. Kozinets 2001. Qualitative inquiry in marketing and consumer research. In D. Iacobucci (ed.), *Kellogg on Marketing*, Chapter 8, pp. 165–194. New York: Wiley.

Silverman, D. 1993. *Interpreting Qualitative Data: Methods for Analysing Talk, Text, and Interaction*. London: Sage.

Silverman, D. 2000a. Analyzing talk and text. In N. K. Denzin and Y. S. Lincoln (eds.), *Handbook of Qualitative Research: Context and Method* (second ed.), Chapter 31, pp. 821–834. Thousand Oaks, Calif.: Sage.

Silverman, D. 2000b. *Doing Qualitative Research: A Practical Approach*. Thousand Oaks, Calif.: Sage.

Silverman, D. 2001. *Interpreting Qualitative Data: Methods for Analysing Talk, Text, and Interaction* (second ed.). Thousand Oaks, Calif.: Sage.

Smith, M. A. and P. Kollock (eds.) 1999. *Communities in Cyberspace*. New York: Routledge.

Stone, P. J. 1997. Thematic text analysis: New agendas for analyzing text content. In C. W. Roberts (ed.), *Text Analysis for the Social Sciences: Methods for Drawing Statistical Inferences from Texts and Transcripts*, Chapter 2, pp. 35–54. Mahwah, N.J.: Lawrence Erlbaum Associates.

Stone, P. J., D. C. Dunphy, M. S. Smith, and D. M. Ogilvie 1966. *The General Inquirer: A Computer Approach to Content Analysis*. Cambridge: MIT Press.

Strauss, A. and J. Corbin 1998. *Basics of Qualitative Research: Techniques and Procedures for Developing Grounded Theory* (second ed.). Thousand Oaks, Calif.: Sage.

Sudweeks, F., M. McLaughlin, and S. Rafaeli (eds.) 1998. *Network and Netplay: Virtual Groups on the Internet*. Cambridge: The MIT Press.

Venables, W. N. and B. D. Ripley 2002. *Modern Applied Statistics with S* (fourth ed.). New York: Springer-Verlag.

Walther, J. B. 1996. Computer-mediated communication: Impersonal, interpersonal, and hyperpersonal interaction. *Communication Research* 23(1): 3–41.

Weibel, P. and T. Druckrey (eds.) 2001. *net_condition: art and global media*. Cambridge: MIT Press.

Weitzman, E. A. 2000. Software and qualitative research. In N. K. Denzin and Y. S. Lincoln (eds.), *Handbook of Qualitative Research: Context and Method* (second ed.), Chapter 30, pp. 803–820. Thousand Oaks, Calif.: Sage.

Weitzman, E. A. and M. B. Miles 1995. *Computer Programs for Qualitative Data Analysis*. Thousand Oaks, Calif.: Sage.

Werry, C. and M. Mowbray (eds.) 2001. *Online Communities: Commerce, Community Action, and the Virtual University*. Upper Saddle River, N.J.: Prentice-Hall.

West, M. D. (ed.) 2001. *Theory, Method, and Practice in Computer Content Analysis*. Westport, Conn.: Ablex.

Wolcott, H. F. 1994. *Transforming Qualitative Data: Description, Analysis, and Interpretation*. Thousand Oaks, Calif.: Sage.

Wolcott, H. F. 1999. *Ethnography: A Way of Seeing*. Walnut Creek, Calif.: AltaMira.

Wolcott, H. F. 2001. *The Art of Fieldwork*. Walnut Creek, Calif.: AltaMira.

Yoffie, A. J. 2002, June. Online focus groups . . . here today, not gone tomorrow. *Quirk's Marketing Research Review* 16(7):20, 92.

Index

F

G

H

I

J

K

L

M

N

O

P